S
OF THE
SCRIPTURES

From Genesis
To Revelation
And the Inter-testament Period

Dr. Gilbert W. Olson

Bride of Messiah Series

DEDICATION
AND
ACKNOWLEDGEMENTS

THIS BOOK IS DEDICATED to the body of Messiah worldwide, and particularly to his bride, that company of believers who love him with all their heart, soul, mind and strength and are endeavoring to leave all sin and become like him who is the exact representation of the Father.

I thank my Father in heaven for calling me to the ministry of being among the many who are calling the company of believers who are the bride of Messiah to get ready for the return of their beloved Bridegroom.

Much of this book is an adaptation of the electronic textbook of House of David Scripture College titled "Survey of the Scriptures." I thank those involved in the writing of it and the administration for permission to use it.

Gilbert Olson

SPECIAL VOCABULARY

IN MY WRITINGS I use some nontraditional words. The reasons for this are in my Bride of Messiah Series, Book One: *Yahushua Messiah, the Last Adam.*

Assembly (church)
Bow down to (worship)
Box of Elohim/Yahuah/the Covenant (Ark of ....)
Elohim, Ĕl (ail), Strong One (God)
  Elohim, a Hebrew word meaning "strong one/s," is commonly translated as
  "God," but is also used for humans, for angels, and for false gods.
Esteem, splendor, honor (glory)
Favor (grace)
Immersion (baptism)
Impale, impaled (crucify, crucified)
Master (Lord)
Messenger (angel) (Gk *angelos* means messenger, whether human or spirit)
Messiah (Christ)
Messianan/s (Christian/s)
Revere, reverence (worship)
Reverence, reverent (godliness, godly)
Scripture/s (Bible)
Set-apart, set-apartness (holy, holiness)
Set-apart spirit, spirit of set-apartness (Holy Spirit)
Sky (heaven/s, when referring to the physical sky)
Slaughter-offering (sacrifice)
Stake (cross)
  Gk *staurós*, Strong's # 4716 "an upright stake, esp. a pointed one."
Yahuah (the LORD, Yahweh, Jehovah)
  Yahuah is the personal name of Elohim. It means "HE IS."
Yahuah Elohim (the LORD God)
Yahushua (Jesus) *Yahushua* means "Yahuah is salvation."
Yahushua Messiah (Jesus Christ)

These words may seem strange at first, but after awhile they should become familiar.

"Son" is capitalized when referring to Messiah. Tradition capitalizes it to show deity; here it is capitalized to show honor.

ALL SCRIPTURE QUOTATIONS are the author's translation unless otherwise noted.

Scripture book abbreviations are as follows:

Gen-Genesis	1Ki-1 Kings	Ecc-Ecclesiastes	Ob-Obadiah
Ex-Exodus	2Ki-2 Kings	SS-Song of Songs	Jon-Jonah
Le-Leviticus	1Ch-1 Chronicles	Is-Isaiah	Mi-Micah
Nu-Numbers	2Ch-2 Chronicles	Jer-Jeremiah	Na-Nahum
Dt-Deuteronomy	Ezr-Ezra	Lam-Lamentations	Hab-Habakkuk
Jos-Joshua	Ne-Nehemiah	Eze-Ezekiel	Zeph-Zephaniah
Jdg-Judges	Est-Esther	Dan-Daniel	Hag-Haggai
Ru-Ruth	Job-Job	Ho-Hosea	Zec-Zechariah
1Sa-1 Samuel	Ps-Psalms	Joel-Joel	Mal-Malachi
2Sa-2 Samuel	Pr-Proverbs	Am-Amos	

Mt-Matthew	2Cor-2Corinthians	1Ti-1 Timothy	2Pe-2 Peter
Mk-Mark	Gal-Galatians	2Ti-2 Timothy	1Jn-1 John
Lk-Luke	Eph-Ephesians	Tit-Titus	2Jn-2 John
Jn-John	Php-Philippians	Phm-Philemon	3Jn-3 John
Ac-Acts	Col-Colossians	Heb-Hebrews	Jude-Jude
Ro-Romans	1Th-1 Thess.	Jam-James	Rev-Revelation
1Cor-1Corinthians	2Th-2 Thess.	1Pe-1 Peter	

TABLE OF CONTENTS

INTRODUCTION

THIS BOOK HAS TWO PURPOSES. The first is to help those who are unfamiliar with the scriptures to become familiar with them. The second is to inspire the reader to go deeper than just this survey.

All scripture is Elohim-breathed and is useful for teaching, for rebuking, for correcting, for training in righteousness, 17 so that the man of Elohim may be thoroughly equipped for every good work (2Ti 3:16).

We each were created to do good works.

For we are his workmanship, created in Messiah Yahushua to do good works which Elohim prepared in advance we should walk in them (Eph 2:10).

The first two books of this Bride of Messiah series give the foundation doctrines of the faith. The first—*Yahushua Messiah, the Last Adam, His Humanity According to Scripture*—proves from scripture that Elohim (God) is one, the Father, that his only begotten Son Yahushua (Jesus) is a human as are all other humans, except without sin, and is not a god-man, and that his spirit is himself and not a third person of himself. This is in contrast with church tradition, which falsely teaches that God is one being in three Persons, called the Trinity, each separate from the other, yet each all of God, and teaches that Jesus, the Second Person of the Trinity, is God who came to earth and became a human so God could die for our sins, thus making him a god-man.

The second book in this series—*The Bride and the Rapture, from Born Again to a Mature Bride*—shows from scripture that the purpose of creation is that Elohim have a people for eternity who love him with all their heart, soul, mind and strength. This is the bride of Messiah for whom Yahuah (the LORD) gave his Son and for whom the Son died. Being born again is the beginning; becoming the bride is the goal. Living the born again life is the path to become the bride. A born again person can lose his salvation along the way and end up in the torment of hell instead of in the blessedness of the presence of Yahuah on the new earth.

1

The 66 Books by Name and Category

THE SCRIPTURES are made up of 66 books, 39 in the Old Testament (OT), and 27 in the New Testament (NT). "Covenant" is a more accurate word than "Testament," but the traditional word is used.

It is good to memorize the names of the books in order, and from time to time to review them in your mind so as not to forget. Also, you should have a reading program in which you read through all the books of scripture regularly, spending at least twenty minutes a day doing so, and not just reading, but thinking about what you read and how to apply it to your life.

Below is an effective method to memorize them. The OT is in five categories, their numbers being 5,12,5,5,12, an arrangement easy to remember. The NT is in seven divisions, their numbers being 5,9,3,1,1,7,1. This arrangement is harder to remember.

OLD TESTAMENT BOOKS (39 books) (5,12,5,5,12, five categories)
The Law (or Five Books of Moses, or Pentateuch), (5 books)
   Genesis, Exodus, Leviticus, Numbers, Deuteronomy.
Historical Books, (12 books)
   Joshua, Judges, Ruth
   1st and 2nd Samuel, 1st and 2nd Kings, 1st and 2nd Chronicles
   Ezra, Nehemiah, Esther
Poetry Books, (5 books)
   Job, Psalms, Proverbs, Ecclesiastes, Song of Songs
Major Prophets, (5 books) (called "Major" because they are long)
   Isaiah, Jeremiah, Lamentations, Ezekiel, Daniel
Minor Prophets, (12 books) (called "Minor" because they are short)
   Hosea, Joel, Amos, Obadiah
   Jonah, Micah, Nahum, Habakkuk
   Zephaniah, Haggai, Zechariah, Malachi
NEW TESTAMENT BOOKS (27 books) (5, 9, 3, 1, 1, 7, 1, seven categories)
Historical Books, (5 books)
   Matthew, Mark, Luke, John, Acts
Letters of Paul to churches, (9 books)

Romans, 1st and 2nd Corinthians
Galatians, Ephesians, Philippians, Colossians
1st and 2nd Thessalonians
Letters of Paul to pastors, (3 books) (called Pastoral Epistles)
1st and 2nd Timothy, Titus
Letter of Paul to a person, (1 book) (called a personal letter)
Philemon
Anonymous Letter, (1 book)
Hebrews (Likely written by Paul)
General Letters, (7 books) (called General because they are to all the church)
James, 1st and 2nd Peter, 1st, 2nd and 3rd John, Jude
Prophecy book, (1 book)
Revelation/Apocalypse

Self quiz: Write down the names of the 66 books in order according to each category.

An Overview of the 39 OT Books

THIS SECTION GOES THROUGH the 66 books giving a brief summary of each.

Old Testament Scriptures (OT) (39 books)

The OT is also called the Tanak. This is an acronym for the three divisions in the Hebrew Scriptures.

> Tanak: The common name of the Hebrew Old Testament. The word is formed, with assistant vowels, from the Hebrew initial consonants of the names of the three divisions of the Old Testament, namely, Torah, the law (the Pentateuch), Nebiim, the prophets, and Ketubim, writings (Hagiographa)
>
> (www.wordnik.com)

The Law (Torah, instruction) (5 books)

Genesis

This is the book of beginnings, from creation to the death of Joseph. It includes the stories of the fall of man, the flood, the lives of Abraham, Isaac, Jacob/Israel and Joseph, and ending with the twelve tribes of Israel settling in the land of Goshen in Egypt.

Exodus

This gives the history of Israel from the death of Joseph to the dedication of the tent (Tabernacle) in the wilderness. It includes Israel becoming slaves in Egypt, Moses leading them out of Egypt through the Red Sea to Mount Horeb, the giving of the Torah (Law), and the construction of the tabernacle (a tent with a wood frame).

Leviticus

This gives instructions on the ceremonial law and duties of the Levites, or priests. The Levites are the tribe of Levi and were set apart to be priests to Yahuah. The book includes instructions of the annual feasts and various offerings.

Numbers

This relates the journey of Israel from Mount Horeb to the Plains of Moab on the east side of the Jordan River opposite the city of Jericho. It includes the census or numbering of the tribes at the beginning and end of the journey, the assignment of land to the tribes, and events in the journey, such as the sending of 12 spies and the false prophet Balaam.

Deuteronomy

The name of this book means "second law." In it Moses gives the Torah to the new generation before crossing the Jordan into the Promised Land. It includes the blessings and cursings regarding obedience to the Torah, the last words and death of Moses, and the appointment of Joshua as the new leader under Yahuah. (The Hebrew spelling of Joshua is the same as for Jesus; namely, Yahushua.)

Historical Books (12 books)

Joshua

This relates the conquest of the Promised Land under the leadership of Joshua. It includes crossing the Jordan on dry land, being circumcised at Gilgal, capturing Jericho, being defeated at Ai (ah-EE), pronouncing the blessings and cursings at Mount Gerizim and Mount Ebal, and the death of Joshua.

Judges (These judges are also called elohim and deliverers.)

This continues relating the conquest of the Promised Land under 13 judges. It has the theme of *"everyone doing right in his own eyes."* Throughout this period Israel repeatedly goes into idolatry. As a result, Yahuah would judge them by sending an enemy nation to oppress them for a number of years. Because of that oppression, Israel would repent of their idolatry, and then Yahuah would send deliverers (judges) to throw off the enemy and to rule for a number of years. This cycle of idolatry, judgment, repentance and deliverance happened many times. The three best known deliverers (judges) are Deborah, Gideon and Samson.

Ruth

The story of Ruth is during the period of the Judges. This woman of Moab, a gentile, becomes the daughter-in-law of the Hebrew woman Naomi, converts to believe in Yahuah as her Elohim, marries Boaz, and is included in the Messianic line.

First Samuel

This gives the story of Israel from the birth of Samuel to the death of King Saul. This includes Saul becoming the first king, ruling 40 years, David being anointed to be the next king, David slaying Goliath, and Jonathan, Saul's son, becoming close friends with David.

Second Samuel

This tells of David's reign of 40 years as the second king of Israel until his death. It includes his becoming king first of Judah, then of all Israel, being tempted by Bathsheba and murdering her husband Uriah (oo-ree-AH), being denounced by Nathan the prophet, and having his son Absalom rebelling against him.

First Kings

This tells of Solomon's reign of 40 years as the third and last king of all Israel, and the reigns of the kings from Solomon to Jehoshaphat of Judah, and Ahaziah of Israel, contrasting those who obeyed Elohim with those who did not. It includes the building and dedication of the temple, Solomon's wisdom and falling into sin, the dividing of the kingdom with 10 tribes in the north (called the northern kingdom, Israel, Ephraim and Samaria) and two in the south (called the southern kingdom and Judah). Well known persons and events during this time are king Ahab and his wife Jezebel, the prophet Elijah and his contest with the prophets of Baal on Mount Carmel, and his anointing of Elisha to succeed him as a prophet.

Second Kings

This covers the reigns of the kings from Ahaziah (of the northern kingdom) and Jehoram (of the southern kingdom) until each kingdom was destroyed and its people taken into captivity. It includes the ministry of Elijah with events such as calling fire down from heaven and his going to heaven without dying, and the ministry of Elisha with his many miracles, such as raising a dead child to life and healing the leper Naaman.

First Chronicles

This is parallel to Second Samuel, but from a priestly perspective. It covers the reign of King David, with some events omitted and some added. It includes the instruction of David to his son Solomon, and his death.

Second Chronicles

This is parallel to First and Second Kings, but from a priestly perspective, with some events omitted and some added. It includes reformations under five kings of Judah (the southern kingdom), the destruction of the temple and Jerusalem by Nebuchadnezzar king of Babylon, the exile of the southern kingdom to Babylon, and the decree of Cyrus the Persian (who had conquered Babylon) for the people to return and rebuild the temple.

Ezra

This tells of the Jews returning from their captivity in Babylon, the rebuilding of the temple, and the inauguration of social and religious reforms. It includes the return of the first group under Zerubbabel authorized by King Cyrus, and the return of the second group under Ezra authorized by King Artaxerxes.

Nehemiah

This has to do with rebuilding of the walls of Jerusalem and the restoration of the Law. It includes the opposition of the Samaritans Sanballat and Tobiah

Esther

This is a story during the period of the captivity in Babylon of a Jewish woman who became queen (wife of King Ahasuerus - Xerxes I) and stopped the plot to destroy all the Jews, leading to the inauguration of the Feast of Purim.

Poetry (5 books)

Job

This is a poetic story of a righteous man whom Elohim allowed to be tested by Satan through much personal loss, physical misery and accusation of three friends. In this trial Job holds steadfast to his faith, although he questions why this is happening to him since he is righteous. In the end he acknowledges that Elohim is all powerful and does everything right, and as a result he is healed and gains more than he had before.

Psalms

This is a collection of 150 poems, mostly by David, some a lament over sin, some giving instruction on how to live righteously, some thanking Elohim for what he has done, and some praising Yahuah for who he is.

Proverbs

This is a collection of moral and religious general rules containing instruction concerning right living. It gives brief teachings on wisdom, justice, self-control, hard work, purity, etc. In these brief sayings a sharp contrast is drawn between wisdom and folly, righteousness and sin.

Ecclesiastes (also called "The Preacher, or The Teacher)

This shows the uselessness (*"vanity, vanity,"* KJV; *"meaningless, meaningless,"* NIV) of trying to find meaning in life through natural thinking and ways.

It includes the saying:

> *To everything there is a season*
> *And a time for every purpose under the sky* (Ecc 3:1).

And it ends with:

> *Let us hear the conclusion of the entire matter:*
> *Fear Elohim and guard his commands,*
> *For this applies to all mankind!"* (Ecc 12:13).

Song of Songs (Song of Solomon)

This illustrates, through a love story, Messiah's love for his bride company of believers, and the growth in maturity of the bride.

Prophetic books.

These pronounce judgment because of sin, and most promise restoration of a remnant because of repentance.

Prophets before the Babylonian captivity

Major Prophets (5 books) (called major because their books are longer)

Isaiah (means Yahuah is savior, or salvation of Yahuah)

He prophesied for 60+ years during the reigns of several kings. He saw the captivity of Samaria (the northern kingdom) by Assyria, warned Judah that they faced a similar fate because of their idolatry, but also gave a promise of restoration to a remnant, and prophesied also against the nations.

It contains many Messianic and end-time prophecies, such as:

For a child is born to us, a Son is given to us,
　　And the government will be on his shoulder.
　　And his name will be called Wonderful Counselor, Mighty Ĕl,
　　Everlasting Father, Prince of Peace (Is 9:6).

We all, like sheep, went astray;
　　We everyone have turned to his own way.
　　And Yahuah has laid on him the sin of us all (Is 53:6) .

All the many (objects) of the sky will be dissolved
　　And the sky rolled up like a scroll;
　　All their many (objects) will fall
　　Like withered leaves from the vine,
　　Like shriveled figs from the fig tree (Is 34:4).

Jeremiah (means raised up or appointed by Yahuah)

He prophesied during the last years of Judah and Jerusalem. He told the people to surrender to Babylon and live, or die if they resist, and he saw the captivity take place because of their sin. He also prophesied against the nations and gave a promise of restoration to a remnant, and said that the captivity in Babylon would last 70 years.

"And you shall seek me and shall find me
　　When you search for me with all your heart" (Jer 29:13).

Lamentations

In five poems Jeremiah laments over the fall of Jerusalem because of the sin of the people; and he prays, repenting of the sin that caused the fall and asks for mercy.

Jeremiah is known as the "weeping prophet."

Ezekiel (means Elohim will strengthen)

He was a captive in Babylon and prophesied of the fall of Jerusalem because of their gross sin. He was also a priest.

He had a vision of four cherubim, each with four faces and four wings.

He acted out many prophesies as signs, like lying on his side for many days.

Yahuah called him a watchman of Israel.

He had a vision of a valley of dry bones that came together and became a great army, representing the restoration of Israel in the Millennium.

Daniel (means Elohim is judge, or judgment of Elohim)

He was a captive who became a wise man in Babylon and interpreter of dreams. He had visions representing world governments, such as a large image of a man. He received information of the last days, called "the seventy weeks of Daniel."

His three friends were thrown into a fiery furnace but without harm. He also himself was thrown into the lion's den and without harm.

He prayed for the end of the captivity, since the 70 years prophesied by Jeremiah was completed.

Minor Prophets (12 books) (called minor because their books are short)

Hosea (means salvation)

He was a prophet to Israel (the northern kingdom) and was a contemporary of Isaiah. Hosea's wife was unfaithful, but he restored her, this being an example of Elohim's love for his unfaithful people Israel.

Joel (means Yahuah is Elohim)

He was a prophet to Judah (the southern kingdom). The occasion of his writing was a locust plague. He prophesied of the Day of Yahuah (Day of the LORD) quoted in Acts about speaking in tongues.

Amos (means burden or burden-bearer)

He was from the southern kingdom, but was a prophet to the northern kingdom.

> *Let justice roll like water,*
> *Righteousness like a strong stream!* (Am 5:24).

Obadiah (means servant of Yahuah)

He prophesied against Edom (descendents of Esau) because they persecuted Israel.

Jonah (means a dove)

He was from the northern kingdom and was told to prophesy against Nineveh, capital of Assyria, that they would be destroyed in 40 days. He ran away from his call and was swallowed by a large fish. While inside he repented, was vomited out on shore, and went to Nineveh. Because the city repented Elohim withheld judgment, which made Jonah angry.

Micah (means who is like Yahuah)

He was from Judah and was a contemporary of Isaiah. He spoke against both Israel (the northern kingdom) and Judah (the southern kingdom). He prophesied about the Messiah:

> *But you, Bethlehem Ephrathah,*
> *Though you are small among the thousands of Judah,*
> *Out of you will come for me one who will be ruler in Israel,*
> *Whose origins are from of old,*
> *From everlasting* (Mi 5:2).

Nahum (means consolation and compassionate)

He perhaps was born in Galilee at Capernaum (which means village of Nahum), but he prophesied from Jerusalem. His prophecy was against Nineveh just before Babylon conquered Assyria.

Habakkuk (means embraced [by Elohim])

He was a contemporary of Jeremiah. He asked Yahuah why the wicked are not judged. The answer: Be patient, judgment will come at its appointed time. However:

> *The just shall live by his faith* (Hab 2:4).

Zephaniah (means hidden by Yahuah)

He was a contemporary of Jeremiah who prophesied against Judah and the surrounding nations.

Prophets after the Babylonian captivity

Haggai (means festive)

His message was a call to the returned remnant in Jerusalem. They had begun rebuilding the temple and stopped. The message from Yahuah was to finish the job.

Zechariah (means Yahuah remembers)

He was a contemporary of Haggai. His writings contain many Messianic prophecies.

> *Rejoice greatly, daughter of Zion!*
>> *Shout, daughter of Jerusalem!*
> *See, your king is coming to you.*
>> *He is righteous and having deliverance,*
>> *Humble and riding on a donkey,*
>> *A colt, a foal of a donkey* (Zec 9:9).

His prophecies contain many visions of the end times in symbolic forms.

Malachi (means my messenger)

He spoke against the remnant for robbing Elohim by giving their worst as offerings. He prophesied of the forerunner of the Messiah.

> *"Behold, I send you Elijah the prophet before the coming of the great and awesome day of Yahuah. ⁶ And he shall turn the heart of the fathers to the children and the heart of the children to their fathers, lest I come and smite the earth with utter destruction"* (Mal 4:5).

(39 books total for the Old Covenant Scriptures)

An Overview of the 27 NT Books

New Covenant Scriptures (27 books in 7 divisions: 5,9,3,1,1,7,1)

History (5 books)

The first three books are called "synoptic gospels" because they are similar in viewpoint and material.

1. Matthew (means gift of Yahuah)

He was a Hebrew tax collector, one of the 12 Yahushua chose to be apostles. His book portrays Yahushua Messiah as king. It has wise men from the east doing homage to the baby Yahushua. Among its many parables is one of ten virgins—five are wise and five are foolish.

In it Yahushua gave the great commission:

"Go therefore and make disciples of all the nations ... I am with you always" (Mt 28:18, 20).

2. Mark (full name: John Mark, half Hebrew and half gentile)

His source of information was Peter, so in a sense this is the Gospel according to Peter. He portrays Yahushua Messiah as servant.

A key word is "immediately." The great commission at the end of the book includes signs that believers will do.

"Go into all the world and proclaim the Good News to all creation. ... These signs will accompany those who have believed: in my name they will cast out demons, they will speak with new tongues" (Mk 16:15,17).

3. Luke

Luke was a gentile researcher and companion of Paul. The book portrays Yahushua Messiah as a man. The book tells of shepherds doing homage to the new-born baby Yahushua and has the parable of the Prodigal Son.

4. John (means gift of Yahuah)

The apostle John is called the one whom Yahushua loved. The book portrays Yahushua as the Son of Elohim and begins with, *"In the beginning was the word"* (Jn 1:1). It shows Yahushua as one with the Father and as an example of what believers in him are to be.

5. Acts of the Apostles

This is a sequel to the Gospel of Luke. It gives the story of the early assembly, beginning in Jerusalem, then Samaria, then the rest of the world. It has Peter (means rock) as the apostle to the Jews, and Paul (means small, little) as the apostle to the gentiles.

Letters of Paul to assemblies (9 books)

1) Romans
This is a general letter on the nature of salvation in Yahushua. Creation witnesses that Elohim exists, so no one has an excuse for unbelief. Only those with the spirit of Messiah belong to him. It shows the relationship of Jews and gentiles in the assembly.

2) 1st Corinthians
This letter deals with moral problems and spiritual authority. It defines what love is and defends resurrection from the dead.

3) 2nd Corinthians
In this letter Paul defends his apostolic authority.

4) Galatians
This letter defends the doctrine of justification by faith and warns against returning to the legalism of Judaism, especially circumcision. Salvation is by faith alone. Works are the result of salvation, not the means. Paul also defends his apostolic authority.

5) Ephesians
This letter shows that Jews and gentiles are together the one body of Messiah. The teachings include that the husband is the head of the wife as Messiah is the head of the assembly, and that the believer should take up the whole armor of Elohim to stand firm in the faith.

6) Philippians
This letter gives thanks for their material help while he was in prison. It calls for unity among believers in the assembly and defines humility, with Yahushua and himself as examples.

> *Let this mind be in you which was also in Messiah Yahushua* (Php 2:5).

7) Colossians
This letter emphasizes Messiah as the head of the assembly.

> *He is the likeness of the invisible Elohim* (Col 1:15).

8) 1st Thessalonians
This was likely the first letter of Paul. It deals with the return of Messiah and being caught up with him in the air (called the rapture).

9) 2nd Thessalonians

This deals with the rapture, saying that first the man of lawlessness (the antichrist) must be revealed.

Pastoral letters (duties of apostles and elders) (3 books)

1) 1st Timothy

There is one Elohim, and one mediator between Elohim and men, the man Messiah Yahushua (1Ti 2:5).

2) 2nd Timothy

Do your utmost to present yourself approved to Elohim, a worker who does not need to be ashamed, rightly handling the word of truth (2Ti 2:5).

All scripture is Elohim-breathed and profitable for teaching, for reproof, for setting straight, for instruction in righteousness, that the man of Elohim might be fitted, equipped for every good work (2Ti 3:16-17).

3) Titus

In all things show yourself to be an example of good deeds, with purity in doctrine, dignified, sound in speech which is beyond reproach, so that the opponent will be put to shame, having nothing bad to say about us (Tit 2:7-8).

Personal letter (1 book)

1) Philemon

This letter tells us that Philemon, who had become a believer through Paul, had a slave named Onesimos. This slave had run away to Rome and had also became a believer through Paul who was in prison, and he became a servant to Paul. Paul sends the slave back to Philemon with this letter and asks Philemon to voluntarily send Onesimos back to be with him.

Anonymous letter, although likely from Paul (1 book)

1) Hebrews

This book shows that Yahushua is the Messiah and, because of all that he did, fulfills all the ceremonial law, thus those laws are fulfilled by living in Yahushua.

> *[The Son] is the radiance of [the Father's] esteem and the exact representation of his nature* (Heb 1:3).

General Letters (7 books)

1) James (half-brother of Yahushua)

This has been called the "Wisdom Book" because of its practical wisdom.

> *For as the body without spirit is dead, so also the faith without works is dead* (Jam 2:26).

2) 1st Peter

Expect suffering as a believer.

> *Those who suffer according to the will of Elohim should commit their lives to a trustworthy creator, in doing good* (1Pe 4:19).

3) 2nd Peter

Warning against false prophets.

> *With Yahuah one day is as a thousand years, and a thousand years as one day* (2Pe 3:8).

4) 1st John

> *Elohim is love, and he who stays in love stays in Elohim, and Elohim in him* (1Jn 4:16).

5) 2nd John

This letter warns against heresy and association with false teachers.

> *And this is love, that we walk according to his commandments* (2Jn 1:6).

6) 3rd John

> *Beloved ones, do not imitate the evil, but the good. The one who is doing good is of Elohim, but he who is doing evil has not seen Elohim* (3Jn 1:11).

7) Jude

Certain men have slipped in whose judgment was written about long ago, wicked ones perverting the favor of our Elohim for indecency and denying the only Master Yahuah and our Master Yahushua Messiah (Jude 1:4).

Prophecy (1 book)

1) Revelation/Apocalypse

This is a book of judgment on the world system, called Babylon, and of warnings to believers to repent so as not to be included in the judgment. At its end we see the wedding of the bride of Messiah; that is, the body of believers who will inherit the new earth.

"Blessed are those who are invited to the wedding supper of the Lamb!" (Rev 19:9)

This has been a very brief overview of the 66 books of the scriptures: 39 in the OT and 27 in the NT.

The names of the books form the "bones" of the whole. The information given with each is like the "meat" on the bones. It is important to have some understanding of each book so that when you think of a book you have some idea of what it is about. The "meat" (or information) given above is very lean. More "meat" is added to the "bones" as we continue.

The Prophetic Seven Days

With Yahuah one day is as a thousand years, and a thousand years as one day (2Pe 3:8).

THIS VERSE is a statement regarding how Elohim Yahuah views history. Elohim created everything in six literal days, and stopped from creating on the seventh day.

The reason he did it in six days and stopped on the seventh is because of his plan for man. That plan is to make a people who love him with all their heart, soul, mind and strength so that they can live with him forever in new bodies on a new earth under a new sky. Elohim created the present universe to be a home for man, but only temporarily. In other words, life on earth is for probation to see who wants to pay the price of self-denial to give up selfishness and commit all to Yahuah. This he planned to accomplish in 7,000 years. In other words, he created the earth and universe at the beginning of the 7,000 years. Its purpose was to be a temporary home for mankind in mortal bodies. After 7,000 years he will burn it up and make a new one to be a permanent home for mankind in immortal bodies (2Pe 3:10-13).

These 7,000 years are divided into seven parts, called dispensations, each approximately 1,000 years.

First day, light (Gen 1:3-5). First millennium: **Adam to Noah**.

By using the length of lives we see recorded in scripture we can see what happened (and what is happening and what will happen) during each of the thousand years. The first millennium, or 1,000-year period, begins with Adam and ends with Noah, 1056 years. Noah's father, Lemech, was 56 years old when Adam died. And Noah was born 126 years after Adam died. This is the antediluvian period, meaning the period before the flood. It was a period that began with great light, and ended with such great darkness that all of mankind except a remnant of eight were destroyed.

Second day, an expanse separates waters above from waters below (Gen 1:6-8). Second millennium: **Noah to Abram.**

In this second millennium we have the world-wide flood, the Tower of Babel in which the languages were confused, and the birth of Abram who would later be called Abraham. It is a period of two separations—the flood (separating those in the ark from those who died), and the tower (groups migrating away from each other because of language differences).

Third day, dry land separated from seas, and seed and fruit bearing vegetation and trees growing on the land (Gen 1:9-13). Third millennium: **Abram to David**.

In this third millennial day—Abraham (2055 B.C.) to King David (1085 B.C.)—we have Abram leaving Ur of the Chaldeans and entering the Promised Land; the lives of Isaac, Jacob and Joseph; the enslavement in Egypt and exodus to the Promised Land; the period of the Judges; and the establishment of the kingdom under King Saul during which time David is born. From this list of events we see separation of peoples and spiritual fruit-bearing in the kingdom.

Fourth day, sun, moon, stars created for seasons and signs (Gen 1:14-19). Fourth millennium: **King David to Yahushua and Pentecost**.

In this fourth millennial day we see the development of the kingdom under David, its division into two kingdoms after his son Solomon, the exile of the northern and southern kingdoms, the return to the Promised Land, apostasy increasing until the birth of Messiah, his ministry of 3½ years to confirm the covenant (with signs and wonders) that was given to Abraham, his resurrection and ascension to receive all authority over heaven and earth, and the outpouring of the set-apart spirit on Pentecost to begin the assembly of Messiah.

Fifth day, sea creatures and birds created (Gen 1:20-23). Fifth millennium: **Pentecost to the Dark Ages.**

In this fifth millennial day we see the assembly spreading throughout the civilized world with signs and wonders to confirm the word, and then quickly compromising with paganism, losing its power, and entering what is called the Dark Ages, a period of political chaos and little education.

The Sixth day, land animals and mankind created (Gen 1:24-31): Sixth millennium: Dark Ages to the return of Messiah to establish his 1,000-year rule.

In this millennial day we see the Renaissance with education increasing, the Reformation of starting to leave Roman Catholic pagan beliefs and practices (starting in 1517 with Luther), the Pentecostal movement (starting in 1901), the charismatic movement (beginning around 1960), and the great apostasy of perverting the gospel (e.g. the prosperity gospel).

We are near the end of this millennial day, in which we will see the birth of the last-day perfected bride of Messiah (Rev 12:5), the rapture of the bride, one world government under the antichrist, in which all remaining believers who refuse to take the 666 mark of the beast will be martyred, the great tribulation on the world, and ending with Messiah's return with his bride to begin his 1,000-year rule.

The Seventh day, Elohim rests (Gen 2:1-3). Seventh millennial day, Messiah returns with his bride, stops the war against Israel and

Jerusalem, throws the antichrist and false prophet alive into hell, binds Satan and his demons in the Abyss (bottomless pit), and rules the earth with his bride for 1,000 years. At the end of the 1,000 years Satan and his demons are released to test mankind (Rev 20:1-3, 7-10).

Types

EVERYTHING that is recorded in scripture has a purpose. That purpose is to make man into the image of Yahuah; that is, to think and act and love the way he does so as to be a people of righteousness. Only a few want to become that image; most do not. Most want to be selfish, which is the likeness of Satan. And so we have in scripture two kinds of people, people of Elohim and people of Satan.

Typology is the study of types. A type is a real person, place or thing that represents something spiritual. That spiritual thing is called an antitype. For example, the first man, Adam, is a type of the last Adam, Yahushua Messiah. Many numbers also have typological meaning. For example, the number four is a type of the world and the universe, because the sun, moon and stars were created on the fourth day and there are four directions: east, west, north and south.

Here is a list of some basic types.

Numbers

4: universal.

5: grace/favor.

6: man.

7: spiritual completeness.

8: new beginnings.

10: completeness in the world.

12: government.

40: testing.

Colors

Blue: heaven(ly).

Red: blood of Messiah, atonement, etc.

Purple: royalty.

Black: sin.

White: purity.

Brown: earthiness, of the earth.

Men: Messiah, anti-messiah, Satan, old man, new man, etc.

Women: assembly, harlot assembly, bride of Messiah.

Landscape

Mountains: problems, barriers; places of spiritual experience.

Valleys: trials, low times.

Oceans: seas, peoples.

Desert: spiritually dry place, place of testing.

Garden: place of Elohim's blessing, fruitful place.

Weather

Storms: judgment, attacks, trial.

Drought: judgment, Elohim withholding the rain.

Rain and dew: blessing, presence of Elohim.

Wind: spirit of Elohim.

Metals

Gold: Elohim.

Silver: atonement.

Bronze or Brass: judgment.

Iron: corruptible, man.

Animals

Sheep versus goats: innocence versus stubborn.

Oxen: ministers, work in the harvest field.

Horse: strength, war.

Dove: the set-apart spirit.

Lamb: Messiah, innocent.

Donkey: man, stubborn.

Locusts: judgment, plagues.

Snake, Serpent: Satan.

Lion: Satan, Messiah.

Dragon (Gk *drakon*, a large snake): Satan.

Nations:

Israel: the assembly, Elohim's people.

Egypt: the world.

Babylon: false religious system.

Trees:

Cedars of Lebanon: proud men.

Hyssop: humble, lowly men.

Fig trees: Jews.

Enemies of Israel:
> Can represent demons, the old man or flesh, sin, the world, etc.

Crops:
> Wheat: spirit-filled, Messiah, elect believers.
>
> Barley: born again, fleshly believers.
>
> Oil: the set-apart spirit.
>
> Wine: blessing of Elohim, joy, refreshing.
>
> Thorns, brambles: unsaved men, enemies of Elohim.

Sky:
> Sun: Messiah, New Testament, sun god.
>
> Moon: Old Testament, moon god.
>
> Stars: believers, leaders.

Also:
> Up versus down: good versus bad.

THIRTYNINE OLD COVENANT BOOKS

FIVE BOOKS OF THE LAW

THIS SECTION lists the main events and persons involved and points out a few examples of typology. It would be *very good* for the reader to read the full account in the scriptures as we proceed through this summary.

1. Genesis

Adam and Eve and the Garden of Eden (Gen 1-3)

THE STORY BEGINS with Elohim creating the world and man. He puts the man in a garden, called the Garden of Eden (and also Paradise), and gives him a wife to be his helper, created from his side. The man's name was Adam, and Adam named his wife Eve (in Hebrew, Ḥawwah, kha-WAH; a dot under the Ḥ/ḥ shows it is a guttural ch, as in Bach). Adam is a type of Yahushua Messiah, and Eve is a type of the assembly and the bride of Messiah. Before they sinned they were in perfect fellowship with Yahuah, and when they sinned they were sent out of the Garden. The Garden, therefore, is a type of communion with Yahuah, and being sent out of the Garden is a type of communion with Yahuah being broken. Because of what Yahushua did, however, those who commit their lives to him inherit the new earth in the next life. This new earth is the antitype of the Garden; it is Paradise restored.

Where was this Garden? Four rivers flowed out from it, two of them have the names of the Euphrates and the Tigris. However, the surface of the land changed at the time of the flood of Noah, so the rivers today with those names are likely not the same as those before the flood.

Adam and Eve both disobeyed Yahuah and were put out of the Garden. Their disobedience was eating fruit from the Tree of the Knowledge of Good and Evil. It was a real tree with real fruit, but with a symbolic meaning. When Adam and Eve were living in perfect obedience to Elohim, he put his will into their minds, and they obeyed without question. They didn't need to think of what is right or wrong. But when they disobeyed, Elohim gave them a conscience, so they had to use their natural minds for deciding what is right or wrong. That is the way mankind has been ever since. Before the fall there was no need for a conscience; after the fall there was a need.

When Lucifer (means light bearer) and the other messengers (angels) were created, they were in heaven with Yahuah. It was their Garden. They were created to be servants of man to help man achieve a higher position than they had (Heb. 1:14). However, because of pride, many hated that plan and rebelled, so they were thrust out, and Lucifer became Satan and the devil, which means adversary and accuser, and his followers became demons. When Adam and Eve sinned, therefore, they chose to be like Satan instead of like Elohim. And so, like Satan, were put out of the Garden. But Elohim gave them animal skins to hide their nakedness. This required the killing of animals, likely lambs. Killing animals was an example of the kind of offering Yahuah wanted. Nakedness is a type of living in sin, clothing is a type of living in righteousness, and the death of animals is a type of Yahushua dying for our sin and covering us with his righteousness. (Think of that every time you eat meat.)

Cain, Abel and Seth (Gen 4)

The whole human race comes from Adam and Eve, and from them

eventually, through a line of descendents, would come the Messiah, the savior of mankind. The first two children of Adam and Eve were Cain and Abel. Cain became a farmer and Abel a shepherd. They learned from their parents the kind of offering Elohim wanted, and it had to be from a right heart motive, a motive of love for Yahuah. One time when Cain and Abel made their offerings to Yahuah, Abel did it the way Yahuah wanted, but Cain did it his own way. He offered grain, the fruit of the labor of his hands, and thought that was good enough. That is a type of doing works to try to gain salvation; but no amount of works can save us (Eph 2:8-10).

When Yahuah rejected his offering, he became angry and killed his brother Abel. In type, therefore, Cain represents the flesh man of selfishness, and Abel represents the spirit man of wanting to please Elohim. Note: the flesh man always comes first. Cain was judged and sent away to be a wanderer. Later, Adam and Eve had another child, Seth. Seth was the one through whom the Messiah would come.

In typology, women represent the assembly, one way or another. In the case of Eve, because of her sons Cain and Abel, she is a type of the assembly producing two kinds of assemblies: the flesh lukewarm assembly, and the spirit fervent assembly totally in love with Yahushua.

Enoch and Methuselah (Gen 5)

The next person of note in Genesis is Enoch, a man who *"walked with Elohim."* He was the seventh generation in the line of Messiah. The number seven in type represents spiritual completeness. He is of note because he was taken by Yahuah without dying. Because of this, he is a type of that company of believers called the Bride of Messiah who will be raptured without experiencing death.

Enoch was the father of Methuselah who is known for having lived the longest, 969 years. The "Adam to Abraham Chart" at the end of this book shows that at the time of the flood they all knew Enoch and the kind of life he lived, and all, except Adam, were living when Enoch was raptured. You will also notice that Noah was born after Enoch was raptured, and Methuselah died in the year of the flood. The flood is a type of the great tribulation and the plagues at the end of the age.

In type, therefore, both Enoch and Noah represent the "hot"

believers who will be raptured (the bride, as noted earlier), and Methuselah represents the "lukewarm" believers who miss the rapture and go into the great tribulation and die. Yahushua said to the Laodicean assembly:

> *"I know your deeds, that you are neither cold nor hot. I wish you were cold or hot!* [16] *So, because you are lukewarm—neither hot nor cold—I am vomiting you out of my mouth"* (Rev 3:15).

Noah and the flood (Gen 6-10)

Mankind was becoming more and more wicked, so wicked that to preserve mankind in order for Messiah to be born, Elohim had to destroy all mankind, except a remnant to begin over again. Noah was the only righteous person in his generation (Gen 6:5-9), and Elohim told him to build an ark (the size of a very large boat) to hold his family and two of every kind of animal, plus some extra to use as offerings.

It took 120 years for Noah to build the ark, and during that time he was preaching righteousness. (See 2 Peter 2:4.) But no one repented of their wickedness. Then Yahuah sent the flood that covered the whole earth and destroyed all mankind and land animals and bird life. The only survivors were Noah, his wife, his three sons, Shem, Japheth and Ham, and their wives—eight in all, plus the animals that came on board.

In this story, in type, Noah represents the bride of Messiah that goes in the rapture without dying, and the flood, as mentioned before, represents the great tribulation on the unrepentant. The number 8 in typology represents new beginnings.

When the flood waters subsided (by land rising and the sea floor sinking) the ark came to rest on the mountain range of Mount Ararat (in present day Turkey).

Then mankind started over again with these eight, with Shem carrying on the Messianic line. Also at this time they were allowed to eat animal flesh. Before the flood they were only allowed to eat vegetables (Gen 9:3). At this time Yahuah gave the covenant of the rainbow, that never again would he destroy mankind by means of a flood (Gen 9:8-16). Before the flood there never had been rain, just a mist that rose from the earth to water the ground.

Nimrod, the Tower of Babel, Babylonian worship (Gen 11:1-9)

Mankind did not learn the lesson of judgment against sin by the flood. The third born of Noah was Ham. Because of wickedness toward his father he was cursed. His grandson, Nimrod (Noah's great-grandson), founded Babylon and built the infamous Tower of Babel. He was a rebel against Elohim. He began again the false religion that Cain started, and after his death he was honored as a god. Because of that religion, Elohim confused their language into several languages and the various language groups migrated apart. All false religions of the earth with all their mythology have their origin in this religion.

Abraham and Isaac (Gen 12-22)

The timeline at the end of this book shows that Abraham was born 57 years before Noah died. So all the people from Noah to Abraham knew about the flood from eyewitnesses. Yet they continued in sin.

Abraham, Isaac and Jacob are known as the Patriarchs of the nation of Israel. Abraham came from Ur of the Chaldeans. (This is different from the Ur in Sumer which is far to the southeast.) By the time of Jeremiah the land of the Chaldeans included Babylonia. This region (and everywhere else) also had the Babylonian system of false worship begun by Nimrod. So Abraham lived in the midst of Babylonian worship at the time Yahuah called him to leave home and go to Canaan, the future Promised Land of Israel.

Babylon means "confusion," "mixture," and "the gate of god." It is a type of the world and the world way of thinking. Because all of us grow up in the world, and because of our in-born tendency toward selfishness, wherever we live on the earth we are in Babylon, and to be born again is to come out of Babylon. For example, Abraham coming out of Ur of the Chaldeans and following Elohim is a type of an unbeliever being converted to Messiah and coming out of Babylon, i.e., out of the world way of thinking. (See 1Jn 2:15-16, which describes this kind of thinking.)

When Yahuah told Abraham to leave Ur, he told him to bring only his wife and to leave his relatives behind. But when he left he brought with him also his father Terah and his nephew Lot and stopped at Haran in Paddan-Aram. This, in type, represents getting born again, but still clinging to some of Babylon in your life. Abraham continued his journey only after his father died. In type, this represents letting a big part of Babylon die in your life. (See Mt 10:34-39 about losing your life for Messiah.)

When Abraham left Paddan-Aram he brought his nephew Lot with him. When they settled in Canaan they both prospered so much as shepherds that they needed to separate. Lot chose the well-watered valley of Sodom and Gomorrah, and Abraham stayed in the hill country. It was after this, after he had separated from all his relatives, that Yahuah promised Abraham that he would be the father of many nations, and that his descendents would be as numerous as the sand on the seashore and as the stars in the sky. In type, this is being called to ministry after fully obeying the Father.

But, as Abraham was getting old and his wife Sarah was barren, he didn't see the promise being fulfilled. So he followed his natural thinking and took Hagar, the slave of his wife Sarah, to be a wife, and had a son by her named Ishmael. But Yahuah said, "No," his descendents would be through Sarah.

It was at this time that Yahuah gave Abraham the covenant of circumcision (Gen 17:10).

We have been using the name Abraham for this man, but originally he was called Abram, which means "exalted father." Abraham means "father of a multitude." It was at this time that his name was changed to Abraham. Also, Sarah's name was originally Sarai, which means "my princess," and at this time her name was changed to Sarah, which means "princess," or "noble woman." (The "...i" at the end of "Sarai" is a suffix that means "my"; thus, "my princess.")

After Yahuah told Abraham this, he told Abraham that he would destroy all the cities in the valley because their wickedness had reached to the full, a wickedness that included gross homosexuality. It is from this wickedness that we get the word sodomy, which means having sex with a person of the same sex.

Abraham begged Yahuah to spare the cities if even as few as ten righteous people could be found there. Yahuah agreed, but there weren't ten. He sent two messengers (angels) to rescue Lot and his family before sending fire and brimstone to destroy all the cities of the valley. The messengers brought Lot and his wife and two daughters out (their betrothed wouldn't come with them), but on their way

26

out Lot's wife looked back longingly at what she had left behind, and she was turned into a pillar of salt as judgment. This, in type, fulfills what Yahushua said:

> *"No one, having put his hand to the plow, and looking back, is fit for the kingdom of Elohim"* (Lk 9:62).

To follow Yahushua we must leave everything of the world behind and love him only.

Because the daughters now had no husbands with whom to have children, each got their father drunk and conceived by him, giving birth to Moab and Ammon. These two offspring became nations that lived east of the Jordan River and gave the nation of Israel much grief.

Thirteen years after the birth of Ishmael, Sarah conceived and bore Isaac, the son of promise. And there was strife between Hagar and Sarah and between Ishmael and Isaac. So Yahuah told Abraham to send Hagar and Ishmael away.

In type, Hagar represents the Old Covenant ceremonial law with its priestly system and offerings, and Sarah represents the New Covenant of salvation in which that ceremonial law is fulfilled through Yahushua Messiah and so is done away. Also in type, Ishmael represents the flesh-man which is hostile toward the Father, and Isaac represents the spirit-man which loves the Father and wants always to obey. This is the same comparison as with Cain and Abel.

Next, to test Abraham's faith, Yahuah told him to offer his son Isaac as a burnt offering on Mount Moriah. Abraham told his son to carry the wood while he carried the knife, and, after tying him on an altar, as he was about to kill him, a messenger of Yahuah told him to stop, and provided a ram instead. In this account, Abraham is a type of Yahuah who offered his son, and Isaac is a type of Yahushua who carried the stake on which he was impaled. The ram is a type of Yahushua also.

The servant of Abraham gets Rebekah as wife for Isaac (Gen 24)

Abraham sent his servant to his relatives in Haran (the city where his father died) to get a wife for his son Isaac. The wife must not come from the local Canaanites (Gen 24:3-6). The servant went to Abraham's nephew in Haran and found Rebekah. She agreed to go back with the servant and marry Isaac without having seen him.

27

In type, the bride of Yahushua must be from the people of Yahuah, not from the world. And the bride position is voluntary. Further, it is the servants of Yahushua, believers in him, who invite people to convert to Messiah without ever seeing him. (See Jn 20:29.)

Jacob and Esau (Gen 25-33)

After being barren for many years Rebekah gave birth to twin boys, Esau (means "hairy") the first born, and Jacob (means "heel holder" or "supplanter"). Esau got his name because he was hairy even at birth, and Jacob got his name because he had a hold of Esau's heel when he and Esau were born. Because Esau was the first born, he had the birthright. But he sold the birthright to Jacob for food when he was hungry. Later, when their father Isaac was old and blind and intended to give the firstborn blessing to Esau, at the command of Rebekah, Jacob, pretending to be Esau, deceived Isaac, and got the blessing instead. When Esau found out, he hated Jacob and plotted to kill him, even though he had already sold the birthright to Jacob. Later, Jacob's name was changed to Israel (means prince of, or contender with, Elohim), and he became the ancestor of the Israelis (which today are called Jews), and Esau became the ancestor of the Arab peoples.

The scriptures say Yahuah loved Jacob and hated Esau (Mal 1:2-3; Rom 9:13). There is a reason for this. Esau represents the flesh man, just as Cain and Ishmael do. And Jacob represents the spirit man, just as Abel and Isaac do. Esau cared more for his stomach than he did for his birthright. His birthright meant nothing to him; he despised it (Gen 25:34). This is the heart of Satan. In contrast, Jacob saw the value of it, and did whatever he had to do to get it. This is the heart of the bride.

When Rebekah heard of Esau's plan to kill Jacob, she convinced Isaac to send Jacob to her home in Haran and get a wife there, and not to get wives from among the Canaanites as Esau had done, wives who had made her life miserable. On his way to Haran Jacob had a dream in which he heard Yahuah give to him the same promises he had given to Abraham regarding his descendents being as numerous as the dust of the earth, and all the nations of the earth would be blessed through him. When he awoke he built an altar and called the place Bethel, which means house of Elohim.

After arriving in Haran, Jacob met Laban, his uncle (the brother of his mother Rebekah) and his two cousins, Rachel the younger and Leah the older. He fell in love with Rachel, and agreed to pay Laban seven years of labor (as a shepherd) to marry her. This was to compensate Laban for the loss of her labor. Because of his love for her, the seven years passed quickly. But Laban deceived Jacob, for when he woke up the morning after the marriage, he found he had married Leah instead. (Laban's excuse was that it was the custom for the older to marry before the younger.) So Jacob worked another seven years to get Rachel. Again, because of his love for her, the seven years passed quickly.

Jacob now had two wives, and also the maids of the two wives as concubines (i.e., servant wives). But he had no property of his own, for all of his work had been paying his uncle to get the two wives. So now he wanted to work to gain sheep and goats for himself. (See the nature of the agreement in Gen 30:31-32.)

Laban agreed. But he and his sons became jealous when Jacob's flocks and herds increased and theirs decreased, for Elohim prospered him. During this time Jacob gained eleven sons and one daughter, Dinah. The last son was Joseph, the only son of Rachel, the wife whom he loved. (The other ten sons were from Leah and the maids of his two wives. Dinah was from Leah.)

Because of that jealousy, Jacob left with his family and possessions (many sheep, goats and servants) to return to his home in Canaan, but he did so secretly leaving at night, because he knew Laban would try to stop him from leaving. Before leaving, however, Rachel, Jacob's beloved, stole the household idols from her father Laban. When three days later Laban discovered what happened he was angry, and with his relatives he pursued Jacob and caught up with him. In a dream, Yahuah had warned Laban not to harm Jacob, but he wanted his household gods back. Jacob said that whoever had them, if any, would die. But after searching all the tents he couldn't find them, because Rachel had hidden them in the camel's saddle and was sitting on them and couldn't get up, because, she said, *"the way of women is with me."* Then Laban left.

Before we go further we need to look at some basic typology. We have already seen that in the account before he left home in Canaan, that Jacob is a type of the spirit-led bride assembly and Esau is a type of the self-led lukewarm assembly. In the account of Jacob, his wives and Laban we see other types.

As to Jacob's marriage, Jacob is a type of Messiah who is looking for a bride whom he loves and who loves him. In type, that is Rachel. He works seven years to get her, which represents the complete spiritual work Yahushua did by dying on the stake for our sins. But he gets Leah instead, who is a type of the lukewarm church. So he works another seven years to get Rachel, which represents the complete spiritual work that the body of Messiah (the assembly) is doing by dying to self and pursuing righteousness and proclaiming the good news so as to bring more into the kingdom and to mature them into becoming the bride. (See Mt 28:18-20 for Messiah's commission to his followers after his resurrection. See also what Paul wrote about this in Eph 5:25-27, 30-32.)

Laban in this account is a type of the world and Babylon, and also of the lukewarm assembly. He is both because the assembly that is lukewarm is that way because they love the world. Also, remember that Haran was located in Babylonia. It is to these people, the luke-warm and the world, that Yahushua comes to get his bride. But the world and the lukewarm do all they can to make it difficult for the bride to leave their way of life.

In the case of Rachel, although she is a type of the bride, her behavior shows that she still clung to some of Babylon. The bride doesn't become mature at once; it takes time to get all of Babylon out of your life. As we shall see later, she dies while giving birth to Benjamin. In type, this is dying completely to self and producing the competed bride.

We now return to the narrative.

Jacob will soon arrive home and meet his brother Esau who, many years before, had vowed to kill him. Being fearful, Jacob prayed to Elohim, and sent his wives and flocks ahead with gifts for Esau with the hope of softening his attitude. That night a man wrestled with him, and in the process dislocated his hip, and changed his name from Jacob to Israel, *"because you have striven with Elohim and with men, and have overcome"* (Gen 32:24-28).

Jacob had changed from being a deceiver (in type, a person living in the flesh nature), to being an overcomer with Elohim (in type, a person living in the spirit nature). Jacob had to struggle hard to change, and this is why Yahuah loved him but hated Esau. For this reason Israel is a type of the bride. From here on he limped, a type of no longer depending on the flesh nature, but trusting Yahuah.

When Israel met Esau, Esau's anger was gone and they embraced. He also had prospered. Esau wanted to help Israel on his way, but Israel declined, and they went their separate ways. In type, the bride does not want spiritual help from those following the flesh nature. That help will always hinder walking in the spirit. We will see this type played out again later.

Dinah (Gen 34-35)

Israel continued south until he came to the city of Shechem. Shechem was also the name of the son of the prince of that city. Dinah, the daughter of Leah, *"went out to see the daughters of the land."* In type, this is believers looking to see what the world is like, and get contaminated. When Shechem saw her, he *"took her and lay with her and humbled"* her. Then his father asked Jacob that she be Shechem's wife, and further, that there be intermarriage between their two groups. (He was thinking that by intermarriage they would get all of Jacob's property.) If Jacob agreed, then that would be the end of Israel as a separate people. (See 2Cor 6:14.)

When Dinah's two brothers of the same mother, Levi and Simeon, heard of it, they were outraged. In revenge they killed Shechem, his father and all the male inhabitants of the city, and rescued Dinah from the city. Then all of Jacob's sons plundered the city, taking everything, including all the livestock and women and children.

After this Elohim told Jacob to go to Bethel and build an altar. This is the place where he had the dream of messengers on a ladder. Before leaving:

> He said to his household and to all who were with him, *"Put away the foreign elohim that are among you, and be clean, and change your garments"* (Gen 35:2).

In type, this is the assembly cleansing themselves of sin and getting garments of righteousness.

Rachel dies giving birth to Benjamin (Gen 35:16-21)

After building an altar to Yahuah at Bethel, while on their way elsewhere, Rachel, Jacob's beloved, died giving birth to Benjamin, her second son. While she was dying she named him Ben-Oni, which means "son of my sorrow." But Jacob named him Benjamin, which means "son of my right hand." Her first son was Joseph.

There are several types regarding this birth. Rachel is a type of the assembly. She had stolen her father's household idols, and Jacob had said that whoever had them would die. This is when she died, and this dying, in type, was her finally dying to self so that something wonderful would happen. That "something wonderful" was her second son, Benjamin.

Her giving birth to Joseph, her first born, is a type of Judaism (the Jewish church) bringing forth the Messiah. Her giving birth to Benjamin, her second born, is a type of the Messianan assembly bringing forth the male son (man child, KJV). This is the last-day bride assembly. We will hear more about both of them later.

Joseph (Gen 37-50)

Thirteen of the last 14 chapters of Genesis are about Joseph. His life has more typology regarding Messiah than any other person in the OT. His name means "Yahuah has added," and Yahushua's name means "Yahuah is salvation." As we go through the outline of his life, we will see the similarity of his life to Yahushua's, and also to the assembly.

Joseph was born of Rachel, the choice one of his father: a type of Yahushua being born of Miryam (Mary), the one chosen by his Father.

Joseph told his father about the wicked things his brothers were doing: a type of Messiah reporting to Elohim what is going on in the assembly.

Israel loved Joseph more than all his children, and showed that love by giving him a special robe: a type of Yahuah loving Yahushua more than any other human, and giving him the spirit without measure.

Joseph's brothers hated him because their father loved him more than he loved them: a type of the Jews hating Yahushua, and also of the flesh church hating the bride assembly.

Joseph had dreams which symbolized his brothers and parents bowing down to him, and his brothers hating him even more for that: a type of the Jews hating the authority of Yahushua, and also of the worldly church hating the spiritual authority of the bride.

Joseph's brothers plotted to kill him: a type of the Jews plotting to kill Yahushua. This is also seen in Cain versus Abel, and Esau versus Jacob.

Joseph's brothers sold him to the children of Ishmael for 20 pieces of silver: a type of Yahushua being sold by Judas for 30 pieces of silver.

Joseph was taken to Egypt and sold as a slave to Potiphar: a type of Messiah being a captive in the world.

Joseph found favor with Potiphar: a type of Yahushua growing in favor with man.

Joseph resisted the temptation of Potiphar's wife to seduce him: a type of Yahushua resisting temptations throughout his life (his temptation in the wilderness is the only recorded one).

When Potiphar's wife falsely accused Joseph of attempted rape, Potiphar believed her and had Joseph put in prison: a type of the Jews turning on Yahushua and crying for his impalement on the stake.

Joseph found favor with the prison warden: again a type of Yahushua growing in favor with man.

Whatever Joseph did, both in Potiphar's house and in prison, Yahuah made it prosper: a type of Yahushua having spiritual success in all he did.

While in prison Joseph interpreted dreams of a cupbearer and a baker, and his interpretations came true in three days—the cup-bearer was returned to his position with Pharaoh, and the baker had his head removed: a type of the word of knowledge in which Yahushua operated.

When Joseph interpreted two dreams of Pharaoh, that there would be seven years of plenty and seven years of famine, and gave advice as to what to do, Pharaoh released Joseph from prison and placed him as second in command over all his kingdom: a type of Yahushua after his ascension receiving all authority over heaven and earth from the Father.

Pharaoh gave Joseph an Egyptian wife: a type of the Father giving Yahushua a bride converted from the world.

Joseph was 30 years old when he stood before Pharaoh: a type of Yahushua being about 30 years old when he began his ministry before Yahuah.

Joseph had two sons, Manasseh (meaning causing to forget) and Ephraim (meaning double fruit): a type of Yahushua forgetting his suffering after his death, and bearing double fruit of souls through his body, the bride assembly.

During the famine *"all the earth came to Joseph in Egypt to buy grain"* (Gen 41:57): a type of people from all nations coming to Messiah through the assembly because of spiritual hunger.

During the famine in Canaan, Jacob/Israel sent Joseph's ten older brothers to Egypt to buy grain (Benjamin stayed home), and they bowed before Joseph: a type of the Father sending the lukewarm church to spirit-led assemblies where spiritual food is.

When his brothers came to Joseph he recognized them, but they didn't recognize him, and he spoke harshly to them: a type of the lukewarm church not recognizing Yahushua when he moves among them, but he knows them and has to speak sternly to them to get their spiritual attention.

Joseph requires his brothers to prove they are not spies by bringing his youngest brother, Benjamin, with them the next time they come for grain: a type of Yahushua not being satisfied with his assembly until the bride is in their midst. (Benjamin is a type of the last-day bride.)

When all the brothers returned, including Benjamin, Joseph had them brought into his house and had a big feast prepared for them: a type of the wedding supper of the Lamb.

During the feast, Joseph gives Benjamin five times as much as any of the others: a type of the bride getting the favor of Yahushua.

The brothers were afraid of Joseph because they had sold him in slavery, but he told them not to be grieved about that *"for Elohim sent me before you to preserve life"* (Gen 45:5): a type of Yahushua being sold to give us life.

Israel and his family come to Goshen in Egypt, 70 in all, counting Joseph and his family. Since they were shepherds and shepherds were an abomination to the Egyptians, Joseph arranged for them to live separate from the people: a type of Messiah arranging the assembly to be separate from the world; also, a type of true pastors of Yahushua being an abomination to the world.

Because of the continuing famine, Joseph buys (with grain) all the silver, livestock, land and lives of the Egyptians for Pharaoh: a type of, by his death, Messiah buying all the world for the Father.

When Israel was about to die, he asked Joseph not to bury him in Egypt but in Canaan where Abraham and Isaac were buried: a type of going to heaven.

Before dying, Israel prophesied over his twelve sons, each one according to his own blessing (Gen 49:1-28): a type of Yahushua choosing the positions of his followers. The prophecy to Judah is fulfilled in Messiah (Gen 49:8-12).

Israel claimed Ephraim and Manasseh, the two sons of Joseph, as his own to be among his tribes. This made 13 tribes. But Levi would be a separate tribe of priests to Yahuah and not receive an inheritance of land in the Promised Land. So this gave Joseph two portions in the Promised Land..

Joseph also prophesied that Elohim would bring all the descendents of Israel out of Egypt and take them to the Promised Land, and told them to bring his bones with them when they come out. This is a type of Yahushua's promise in John 14:1-3.

2. Exodus

THE BOOK OF EXODUS gives the account of the Hebrews, under the leadership of Moses, being delivered from slavery in Egypt and receiving the Law (Torah, Instructions) of Yahuah at Mount Horeb (also called Mount Sinai). The law included erecting the Tent of Meeting (also called Tabernacle).

What follows is the overall typology of the journey from Egypt, to Mount Sinai, to the Jordan River, and finally into Canaan, which is the Promised Land. This typology covers from the book of Exodus to the book of Deuteronomy. The whole of it is a type of the journey of salvation.

- Egypt is a type of the world and being enslaved to sin in the world.
- The Passover, just before leaving Egypt, is a type of being born again.
- Crossing through the Red Sea is a type of water immersion (baptism).

- The hardships on the way from the Red Sea to Mount Sinai are a type of the trials we go through after being born again, to test our commitment and salvation.
- The giving of the Torah (Law) on Mount Sinai is a type of being filled with the set-apart spirit at Pentecost and having the Law written in our hearts.
- The wanderings in the wilderness from Mount Sinai to the Jordan River across from the Promised Land is a type of more trials after immersion in the spirit to test our commitment and salvation.
- Those of the generation who left Egypt (20 years old and upwards) who died in the wilderness before reaching the Promised Land are a type of lukewarm believers who lose their salvation and don't enter the eternal kingdom.
- Those of the new generation who reached the Promised land (under 20 years old when leaving Egypt and those born along the way) are a type of the bride of Messiah who keep their salvation and who do enter the eternal kingdom.

With these types in mind, we will look at some select events in the book of Exodus. We will see the flow of history as well as some of the typology involved.

Yahuah tells Moses to deliver the Hebrews (Ex 1-4:28)

The account starts with the Hebrews increasing greatly in population and a new Pharaoh who doesn't acknowledge the value of what Joseph did to save the people of the land. The new Pharaoh is fearful that the Hebrews will become strong and take over the nation, so he makes them all slaves. The hardship of this slavery causes the Hebrews to cry out to Elohim for deliverance. Spiritually, it is when people are in trouble that they cry out to Elohim.

To try to control the Hebrews the new Pharaoh ordered that the midwives kill all males at birth, but they ignored the rule. Three months after Moses was born, because they could no longer hide him, his mother hid him in an ark (basket that could float) which she placed among the reeds by the edge of the river. Pharaoh's daughter found him and decided to keep him. She had him raised first by his mother to nurse him, and then in the palace as her son. So Moses grew up in the palace, but knew who he really was. In type, this is Messiah who grew up in the world, but knew Yahuah was his Father.

Moses hated that his fellow Hebrews were slaves, and one day (he was 40) when he saw an Egyptian beating one of his brothers, he killed and buried him, thinking that no one saw him do it. (In type, this is doing ministry out of your own natural thinking.) But Pharaoh heard about it and sought to kill him, so he fled to Midian. This land was on the east side of the Gulf of Aqaba in what is now Saudi Arabia. These people were the descendents of Abraham by Keturah. He married her after his wife Sarah died. So they were relatives of Moses in the same way that the descendents of Ishmael were.

In Midian, Moses met Jethro, married his daughter Zipporah, and worked as a shepherd for forty years. One day while shepherding by Mount Horeb, a messenger of Yahuah appeared to him in a flame of fire from in a bush. He was now 80 years old. In that experience Yahuah told him to bring his people, Israel, out of Egypt, and gave him a sign that he should bring them to this mountain. He also told him that his name is Yahuah (Ex 3:10,12,15).

Note two things in this experience: 1) He would bring the children of Israel to that very mountain in Midian, called both Mount Horeb and Mount Sinai (and thus not to the traditional site in the Sinai Peninsula). 2) Elohim's personal name is Yahuah, and it is to be remembered. Yahuah's name is used over 6,000 times in the OT, plus numerous times when used as part of peoples' names.

Moses made excuses for not wanting the job, including that he was a poor speaker. Note: excuses don't work with Elohim. Anyway, to help Moses, Yahuah sent his older brother, Aaron, to be his mouthpiece, and that Moses would be an elohim to him (Ex 4:16). In this type, Moses represents Elohim and Aaron represents Messiah, for it is Messiah that tells us the Father's will.

Moses in Egypt and the 10 plagues (Ex 4:29- 13:22)

When Moses came to Egypt and told the children of Israel the good news, that Yahuah their Elohim was going to free them, they were very happy. But when he told Pharaoh to let Yahuah's people go, Pharaoh increased the burden on the slaves, and they complained to Moses and no longer believed him. But Yahuah had set the situation up knowing what Pharaoh would do, and what he, Yahuah, would do as a result. (See Ex 7:1-5; 9:16.)

It is through signs and wonders that Yahuah demonstrates to the people of the world that he is Elohim, and there is no other. For us today, signs and wonders are to be a second witness to confirm the Good News of Yahushua Messiah; but they are also a pronouncement of judgment on those who refuse to believe. In the case of Pharaoh, the signs and wonders were judgments on their gods, to show that they are nothing and that Yahuah alone is Elohim. Yahuah sent ten plagues as judgments, but spared his people living in Goshen from the last seven (Ex 8:22).

The plagues were: 1) water becomes blood, 2) frogs all over the land, 3) gnats, 4) flies, 5) livestock die, 6) boils, 7) hail, 8) locust, 9) darkness, 10) death of the firstborn.

The tenth plague has to do with the Passover. These are the instructions to prevent their own firstborn from dying: (1) This month (beginning with the new moon) would begin the new year. (In their calendar all months began with a new moon.) (2) On the 10th day of this month each household would choose a perfect one-year-old male lamb (or a goat kid) and keep it until (3) the 14th day, at which time they would *"kill it between the evenings."* (Exo 12:6); that is, between noon and sunset. In practice it would be around 2-3 pm in today's clock time. (See Ex 12:7-13 for the instructions.) It had to be early enough in the afternoon so as to accomplish everything else that must be done. This is the time of day in which Yahushua was impaled on the stake.

After this last plague, Pharaoh told the children of Israel to leave, and the Egyptians urged them to go and gave them much wealth. Elohim led them by way of the wilderness, in a column of cloud by day and a column of fire by night (Ex 13:17-18, 20-21).

Crossing the Red Sea (Ex 14:1 - 15:21)

This map shows their route. They stopped when they came to the Gulf of Aqaba and were trapped. Pharaoh and his servants had a change of heart and overtook them. Then the children of Israel, thinking they were all going to be killed, complained to Moses, saying it was better to serve Pharaoh.

In type, this is new believers who find themselves facing big trials they never experienced before. The purpose of trials is to test the hearts, to find out who are the true believers; that is, who are the bride of Messiah.

But Yahuah moved the cloud that was leading Israel so that it was between Israel and Pharaoh, stopping Pharaoh and his army. Then Yahuah divided the sea, the children of Israel crossed over on dry ground, Pharaoh's army followed, the sea returned, and his army drowned.

(map from wyattarchaeology.com/red_sea.ht)
(Scripture doesn't say that Pharaoh himself drowned with his army. bibletools.org/index.cfm/fuseaction/Library.sr/CT/BQA/k/102/Did-Pharaoh-of-Exodus-Drown-in-Red-Sea-Exodus-1428.htm.)

Trials on the way to Mount Horeb, Manna (Ex 15:22- 18:26)

The Hebrews rejoiced at their deliverance, but quickly grumbled at Moses again when they ran out of water and, when reaching Marah, the water was too bitter to drink. This was another test from Yahuah. Then Yahuah showed Moses a tree, which he threw into the waters and *"the waters were made sweet"* (Ex 15:25).

The next trial Yahuah gave was lack of food. So the people grumbled, and Yahuah provided a miraculous grain, called manna (it means "what is it"), and quail. Regarding the manna, for five days Israel had to gather only enough for one day, and on the sixth day, because they were forbidden to gather on the sabbath (Ex 16), they had to gather enough for two days.

When the people grumbled again because of no water, Moses struck a rock in Horeb, and water came out (Ex 17). The rock is a type of Messiah, and striking it is a type of Messiah being impaled for our sins. Even as Messiah died once for all, so the rock must be struck only once. Numbers 20 records a similar grumbling because of lack of water, but that time Moses is told to speak to the rock.

In the next trial Amalek (descendents of Esau), without provocation, came and fought with Israel in Rephidim, a type of the flesh-man attacking the spirit-man, the same as with Cain and Abel, Ishmael and Isaac, and Esau and Jacob. Keep in mind that Israel had been in slavery to Egypt for generations and had no training in war, whereas the nomadic tribes, such as Amalek, thrived in fighting one another. To win, Moses put Joshua in charge of selecting and leading an army, while he stationed himself on top of the hill with the rod of Elohim in his hand, and Aaron and Hur with him.

> *And it came to be when Moses held up his hand that Israel prevailed. And when he let down his hand Amalek prevailed* (Ex 17:11).

So Aaron and Hur supported his hands, and Joshua defeated Amalek. The spiritual lesson: pray for our assembly leaders so as to win battles against the enemy.

Because Moses was the leader of Israel and heard from Elohim, the people were coming to him to decide cases and solve problems. But the people were so many that he was getting worn out, and the people themselves were getting worn out from standing in line all day. When Jethro, his father-in-law, came to visit him, he advised Moses to get wisdom from Elohim and teach the people how to behave among themselves, and he should appoint able men who fear Elohim to be rulers of thousands, rulers of fifties, and rulers of tens and for them to judge the cases, with only the most difficult cases being brought to him. This is a type of delegating authority in the assembly.

The Law given at Mount Horeb (Ex 19-24)

We now come to the giving of the Torah (Law) at Mount Sinai, and particularly the Ten Words (Commandments). These are the Ten Words: Exodus 20:3-17.

1. Have no other elohim (mighty ones, gods) before me (20:3).
2. Do not make for yourself a carved image, or any likeness of that which is in the sky above, or which is in the earth beneath, or which is in the waters under the earth (20:4).
3. Do not bring the name of Yahuah your Elohim to nothing (20:7).
4. Remember the sabbath day to set it apart (20: 8).
5. Respect your father and your mother (20.12).

6. Do not murder (20:13).
7. Do not commit adultery (20:14).
8. Do not steal (20:15).
9. Do not bear false witness against your neighbor (20:16).
10. Do not covet (20:17).

The laws of the seventh day sabbath include giving the work animals and servants rest. And the land should also have rest every seventh year, meaning no plowing, planting or harvesting. Whatever grows naturally is for the poor and the animals.

Yahuah also instituted three annual festivals, at which time all adult males were to appear before the Master Yahuah.

1. The Festival of Unleavened Bread. This occurs at the time of the barley harvest and is preceded by Passover. This feast is a type of being born again, or salvation.
2. The Festival of Harvest, also called Festival of Weeks and Pentecost. This occurs at the time of the wheat harvest and is a type of being spirit-filled.
3. The Festival of the Ingathering, also called Tabernacles and Booths. This occurs at the time of the fruit and nuts harvest. It is the last harvest of the agricultural year and is a type of the completed bride of Messiah and the rapture.

The seventh year rest of the land and the three festivals were laws that would go into effect when they entered the Promised Land and became resident farmers.

When Moses was with Yahuah on the Mount for 40 days, the people grew impatient and told Aaron to make mighty ones (elohim, idols) to lead them. Aaron told them to give him their gold earrings, and from these he made a molded calf. This would be like the golden calf the Egyptians bowed to, and they called it their elohim who brought them *"out of the land of Egypt!"* (Ex 32:4). Then Aaron built an altar before it and held a festival to Yahuah the next day. And what a day it was! After doing the religious part of offering animals and feasting, they *"rose up to play."* This "play" was a wild party with drunken music, dancing and sex. This is a type of an assembly going astray when it lacks spirit-led authority.

Meanwhile, up on the mount, Yahuah gave Moses two tablets of stone on which Yahuah wrote the Ten Words. And he told Moses what was going on down below and that he, Yahuah, wanted to make an end of them and make of Moses a great nation. But Moses interceded for them, and Yahuah relented. Of course, Yahuah said what he said so that Moses *would* intercede. In other words, he did it for the sake of Moses, that he would learn the heart of Yahuah. In this, Moses is a type of Messiah who intercedes for his assembly.

When Moses came near the camp and saw what was going on, he threw down the tablets and broke them, burned the calf they had made, ground it into powder, mixed the powered gold with water, and made them drink it (Ex 32:19-20).

Then, when Moses asked who was for Yahuah to come to him, the sons of Levi gathered to him, and he told them to kill each one his friend and relative. About 3,000 men died that day (Ex 32:27-28). Yahuah himself also sent a plague on the people involved in the sin. This is a type of judgment on rebels in the assembly by spirit-led leaders of the assembly, without which the whole assembly would be destroyed.

Later, Yahuah again called Moses to the Mount where he was for 40 days and 40 nights without food or water. There he wrote again the Ten Words of the covenant on stone tablets. And when he came down, his face was shining so brightly that he had to cover his face with a veil (Ex 34:28-35).

The Tabernacle (Ex 25-40)

Then Moses gave them instructions on making the Dwelling Place, or Tabernacle, on making the furniture for the Dwelling place, and on

making Aaron's garments as high priest. And it all was completed.

This picture is a represen-tation of what the tabernacle complex looked like. It shows a rectangular tent facing east, surrounded by a fence with a gate, and with two objects in front of it. The complex and

everything connected with it represent salvation. The gate represents entering salvation from the east (a type of Babylon and the world) through

42

being born again. The two objects in the outer court are the bronze altar and the bronze basin or laver.

The tent itself is the Tabernacle proper: 10 cubits wide, 10 cubits high, and 30 cubits long. (A cubit is about 18" to 22" inches.") It had two rooms separated by a curtain, or veil. The first room is called the Set-apart Place (or Holy Place, 10 cubits wide and high and 20 cubits long); and the second room is called the Most Set-apart Place (or Holy of Holies, 10 cubits each direction, a perfect cube). Here is some typology.

Outer Court = First step of salvation/ born again.

> Bronze altar = Messiah's offering himself for sin/ our daily dying to self.
>
> Bronze basin/ laver = water immersion/ cleansing our walk in the world.

Set-apart Place = Second step of salvation/ immersion in the Set-apart Spirit.

> On the right or north, the Table of Showbread = sustenance in Messiah.
>
> On the left or south, the Golden Lampstand = revelation light/ walking in the spirit.
>
> In front of the Veil, the Gold altar of incense = worship/ prayer/ intercession.

Most-Set-apart Place = Union with the Father and Son.

> Box (Ark) of the Covenant = Yahuah's provision for fellowship.
>
> Lid of atonement = Yahuah's presence.

Of special interest is the Box of the Covenant (a wood box overlaid with gold) and the lid of the Box made of solid gold. In the Box were three objects: 1) the two tablets of stone on which were engraved the Ten Words (Yahuah's covenant with man) given by Yahuah to Moses on Mount Horeb, 2) a pot of manna (a memorial of Yahuah's provision), and 3) Aaron's rod that budded (representing Yahuah's delegated authority through leadership appointed by him). Yahuah's presence was symbolized by a pillar of cloud by day and a pillar of fire by night that rose from the Box of the Covenant.

When the Tent of Meeting (Tabernacle) was finished and dedicated, Yahuah's presence was manifested in a cloud (Ex 40:34-38). This is what we are desiring for the assembly, that Yahuah's presence comes in our midst so powerfully that we are unable to minister, but just reverence him.

The Book of Exodus ends with the completion of the Tent of Meeting.

3. Leviticus

THIS BOOK CONTINUES with the instructions regarding the Tent of Meeting, responsibilities of the priests, various offerings and various other laws on behavior and punishments for disobedience. The laws also include what is ceremonially clean and unclean. But there are also some historical events that happened. These are what we will look at next. The first is in **chapter 10** regarding two sons of Aaron.

Nadab and Abihu (Lev 10)

These two sons brought incense before Yahuah not according to the way he had commanded them, called "strange fire," and fire went out from Yahuah and consumed them and they died (Lev 10:1-2).

"Strange fire" refers to fire not authorized by Yahuah. This was a sin of presumption. They wanted to lift themselves up in the priesthood without being called by Yahuah, but what they did was unacceptable. This is a type of people entering the ministry out of their own mind without being called by Elohim.

The Day of Atonement and the Festivals (Lev 16-23)

Chapter 16 gives instructions regarding the Day of Atonement. Many rules are given regarding what the priests and people are to do. Among them is this: On the tenth day of the seventh month no one is to do any work, it is a special sabbath, for the priest is to make atonement for himself and all others (Lev 16:29-31).

The first month has Passover and the Feast of Unleavened Bread. The tenth day of the first month they were to select a lamb (or baby goat) for offering. That lamb is a type of Messiah being selected for execution. The Day of Atonement is also on the tenth day, seven months later, and precedes the Feast of Booths (or Tabernacles). Yahushua fulfills this day, for he is our atonement for sin.

Chapter 23 lists the appointed times of Yahuah as special set-apart gatherings (v. 2). They are as follows:

1. The regular weekly sabbath, do no work.

2. Passover, the 14th of the first month. This varied as to the day of the week each year.
3. Feast of Unleavened Bread. This lasts seven days, starting on the 15th of the first month. No work on the first and last days of the feast.
4. Feast of Weeks, also called Pentecost. This is seven sabbaths after Passover, or 50 days. A one day feast, no work.
5. Feast of Trumpets, on the first day of the 7th month, no work.
6. Day of Atonement, on the 10th day of the 7th month, no work, starting from the evening of the 9th day.
7. Feast of Booths, lasts seven days plus one, starting on the 15th day of the 7th month, no work on the first day and 8th day of the feast.

Note, the days of "no work" are also called sabbaths. They are special or high sabbaths. Note also that their days began and ended at sunset. Because Yahushua is the fulfillment of Passover, we will look at the chronology from his death to his resurrection in the year that it took place. Yahushua said:

> *"For as Jonah was in the belly of the huge fish three days and three nights, so the Son of Man will be in the heart of the earth three days and three nights"* (Mt 12:40).

According to our calendar, the day of Passover in the year Yahushua was impaled was a Wednesday. He was impaled about noon and buried before sunset. This timing was to give people time to get home before the special sabbath of the first day of Unleavened Bread, which began at sunset.

The following day (starting at sunset of our Wednesday and ending at sunset of our Thursday) was the special sabbath of the first day of Unleavened Bread, in which no work could be done. That is why the Jews wanted Yahushua buried before sunset on our Wednesday. So, before sunset of our Thursday, he was in the grave one full day and one full night, or 24 hours.

The next day (starting at sunset of our Thursday and ending at sunset of our Friday) was the 2nd day of the Feast of Unleavened Bread, and work *could* be done. This was when the women could buy spices for bringing to the tomb. So, before sunset on our Friday, Yahushua was in the grave two full days and two full nights, or 48 hours.

The day after that (starting at sunset of our Friday and ending at sunset of our Saturday) was the 3rd day of the Feast of Unleavened Bread, and also the regular weekly sabbath, or 7th day of the week, and work was again forbidden. So, before sunset on our Saturday Yahushua was in the grave three full days and three full nights, or 72 hours. So Yahushua could have risen from the dead a little bit *before* sunset on our Saturday.

Finally, the next day (starting at sunset of our Saturday and ending at sunset of our Sunday) was the first day of the week. It was on the first day of the week in the morning that the women came to the tomb, and Yahushua had already risen, likely six hours before they got there. So, contrary to church tradition, Yahushua was *not* crucified on a Friday and did *not* rise from the dead the following Sunday at sunrise. That tradition came from Babylonian sun-god worship that had come into the church.

Except for the weekly sabbath, these "appointed times" can be placed in three groupings.

1. Passover and the Feast of Unleavened Bread. They are in the first month, and it is the time of the barley harvest. This feast was fulfilled when Yahushua was nailed to a stake, and is a type of being born again.
2. Feast of Weeks. This is fifty days after Passover (thus the Greek word Pentecost), and it is the time of the wheat harvest. This feast was fulfilled at Pentecost, and is a type of being immersed in the spirit.
3. Feast of Booths. The feast itself begins on the 15th day of the 7th month, but is preceded by the Feast of Trumpets on the first day and the Day of Atonement on the tenth day. This month is the time of the nut and fruit harvest. This feast is soon to be fulfilled and is a type of the rapture of the completed Bride.

The Year of Jubilee (Lev 25)

Chapter 25 repeats information about the sabbatical year, and introduces the Year of Jubilee. Every seven years they were to let the land lie fallow; that is, not plowing, planting and harvesting, and not even pruning the vines, but just eat what grows of itself. The Year of Jubilee is the year following seven of those sabbatical years, making it the fiftieth year. That year the land was also to lie fallow, making two years in a row of not working the farm, but just eating what grows of itself. The people during those years were to trust Yahuah to provide for them. They would expect a large enough harvest in the year before so as to last through the sabbatical year and the Year of Jubilee.

The Year of Jubilee would begin with the blowing of a shophar (ram's horn) throughout the land on the Day of Atonement; that is, on the tenth day of the seventh month. It was also a proclamation of release, for everyone was to return to his possession and to his clan.

> Whenever a piece of land was sold, the proximity of the next Year of Jubilee determined the price, for this determined how much produce the new owner could get from the soil. Since the buyer knew full well that the land would eventually revert back to the original owner, he certainly wasn't going to pay more for the land than what he would be able to get out of it. "The land shall not be sold forever" was God's law (Lev 25:23).
>
> These laws made it impossible for ruthless wealthy real estate speculators to accumulate vast land holdings and thus upset the economy. Even the poorest Israeli family received its land back, and by working the land, they could gain enough wealth to meet their needs and perhaps the needs of others. The Year of Jubilee provided a new beginning for the released slaves and the landowners, and this kept poverty and inequality to a minimum. The people were not to oppress one another (v. 17), but remember that the land was God's and they were only His tenants (vv. 23-24).
>
> (The Bible Exposition Commentary: Old Testament © 2001-2004 by Warren W. Wiersbe. All rights reserved.)

This was a good law. The problem is, they never obeyed it after they entered the Promised Land, not even once.

The Jubilee is a type of the Millennium for Jews, and a type of the new sky and new earth for all believers, for then is when the full release comes.

4. Numbers

THIS BOOK counts the people Israel, the 12 tribes, and completes the story of the journey from Mount Sinai to reaching the east side of the Jordan. Did they learn their lesson to trust Yahuah and gladly obey his instructions given through Moses, or did they grumble when trials came? The answer is sad. But it is also the answer of the vast majority who call themselves Christian. Israel on their journey through the wilderness is a type of a believer on his journey from being born again to becoming part of the bride of Messiah; and it is also a type of the assembly of Messiah from its birth at Pentecost to its perfection in the last-day mature bride assembly. In Israel's journey, of those 20 years old and older who left Egypt, all but two, Joshua and Caleb, died in the wilderness and didn't make it. It is a story of one rebellion after another, each receiving its judgment, but no repentance. So it is with those who get born again: only a few will enter the eternal kingdom.

Judgment by fire (Num 11:1-2)

When the fire of Yahuah burned among them, the people cried out to Moses, and when Moses prayed to Yahuah, the fire died down. This is a type of praying for those who are backslidden and are losing their salvation.

Judgment by quail (Num 11:33)

Some Egyptians had joined Israel when they left Egypt, so that they were a mixed multitude. In type, these are people who join the assembly but never get born again. They began complaining about the manna. They were tired of it and wanted meat along with all the vegetables, like they had in Egypt. And more and more of Israel joined them in that complaint. The spiritual lesson in this is that complaining in an assembly will gradually infect everyone in it, so that the assembly is destroyed.

Moses brought the problem to Yahuah, and Yahuah brought a judgment of quail. They wanted flesh, and he gave it to them, and Yahuah smote them with a great plague.

Miryam becomes leprous (Num 12:8)

Miryam and Aaron, older sister and brother of Moses, thought that they had equal authority from Yahuah with Moses. So Yahuah called them to the Tent of Meeting along with Moses, and told them they were wrong to speak against Moses and should be afraid to do so. As a result, Miryam became leprous, and she had to be shut out of the camp for seven days before she could come back. This incident teaches that speaking against Yahuah's appointed servant deserves punishment. It is rebellion against authority—authority established by Yahuah, and therefore rebellion against him—and if allowed to go on will destroy the assembly.

The 12 spies and their evil report (Num 12-14)

Twelve men, one from each tribe, were sent into the Promised Land (Palestine) to see what the land and people were like. When they returned after 40 days, they reported that the produce of the land was wonderful, but the people of the land were giants with great walled cities, so no way could they go in to conquer the land. Two of them, Joshua and Caleb, agreed with the abundance of the land, but said indeed they could conquer the land, because Yahuah was with them. But the word of the ten others convinced the people, so that all the congregation lost heart and wanted to go back to Egypt, and even wanted to stone Moses.

As a result, Yahuah wanted to destroy them for their rebellion and start over with Moses, as he did earlier on account of the golden calf, but again Moses interceded. As a result, Yahuah declared that not one of the whole generation who left Egypt, 20 years old and above, would enter the Promised Land, except Joshua and Caleb, but all would die in the wilderness. Only the new generation would enter. Then the ten with the bad report died by the plague before Yahuah (Num 14:31-37).

This is a type of the new generation coming into the kingdom in the revival of the last-days, but much of the older generation will not.

But did the congregation listen and accept the punishment? Not at all! They decided that they would go into the Promised Land right then and not wander and die in the wilderness. So, by faith in their own might, and in rebellion against Yahuah, an army of them rushed into Palestine, and were all killed by the inhabitants.

Korah and his band (Num 16)

This is another example of rebellion against the leadership Yahuah has chosen, and the result. Korah, of the tribe of Levi and thus in the priestly line, gathered together 250 leaders of Israel, telling them that the whole assembly is set-apart, and Moses and Aaron are no better than they (Num 16:3), and who were they that they should rule?

Actually, Moses didn't want the job and tried to reject the calling, but Yahuah thrust it on him anyway. Yahuah always works through delegated authority from the top down in a pyramid structure. And those who try to usurp authority do so to their own destruction, and must be removed from the assembly or else the whole assembly will be corrupted and destroyed.

At the direction of Yahuah, Moses told the congregation to move away from the rebels and their tents. Then the earth opened up and swallowed Korah and his household, and fire from Yahuah consumed the 250 who were offering incense (Num 16:31-35).

Instead of repenting, however, the congregation blamed Moses and Aaron for the death of these people (as though Moses had the power to open the earth or send fire). So Yahuah sent a plague against them to destroy them all. The account doesn't say what the plague was, but evidently it was a plague of sudden death, advancing like a wave, and it was only stopped by Aaron. Moses told Aaron to take incense and make atonement for the people. He stood between the dead and the living and the plague stopped. 14,700 people died from the plague, besides Korah and the 250 leaders (Num 16:46-50). This is a type of intercession for forgiveness of sin.

Aaron's rod buds (Num 17)

Chapter 17 records the account of Aharon's rod budding. Yahuah wanted to show the congregation whom Yahuah Elohim, the creator of heaven and earth, had chosen, so that there would no longer be any doubt. So he called for a leader of each tribe to have a rod (a staff made from an almond tree) and to write his name on it and place it in the Tent of Meeting before the Witness (referring to the Box of the Covenant). The one whose rod budded would be the one whom Yahuah had chosen. The next day when Moses brought out the rods, only Aaron's had budded. As a reminder of this miracle, Aaron's rod was put in the Box of the Covenant along with a sample of manna and the stone tablets with the Ten Words (Num 17:8-10).

Moses strikes the rock twice (Num 20)

In chapter 20 we have the third account of the congregation grumbling because of no water; the first two were recorded in Exodus before they came to Mount Horeb. In the first account the bitter water was made sweet by throwing a tree into it. In the second account Yahuah told Moses to strike the rock at Horeb, and water flowed out. This time Yahuah told Moses to speak to the rock. But, in frustration and anger at the people for their constant complaining, he struck the rock instead, breaking the type of Messiah who was impaled only once, and his punishment was that he would not be allowed to bring Israel into the Promised Land (Num 20:9-12).

This does not mean Moses lost his salvation. To fulfill a certain type, it was necessary that he not lead the congregation into the Promised Land, but that Joshua be the one. In this typology, Moses is a type of Messiah who, by dying, provides salvation and begins the assembly; and Joshua is a type of the believers who are the bride of Messiah that leads the assembly into maturity.

As Israel continues on their way, they ask Edom (descendents of Esau) for permission to pass through their land (an area southeast of the Dead Sea) (Num 20:17). But Edom refuses permission.

It was at this time that Aaron died and his son Eliezer took his place as high priest.

Judgment by fiery snakes (Num 21:5-8)

Later, when the people grumbled again against Elohim and Moses for lack of food and water and being tired of the manna for food, Yahuah sent fiery snakes among them to bite them, and many died. As a result, the people confessed their sin and asked Moses to pray for them. Moses did so, and Yahuah told him to make a fiery snake and set it on a pole, and everyone who was bitten who looked at it would live.

The snake on a pole is a type of Messiah bearing our sin when he was impaled on a stake and lifted up. Yahushua, referring to this event, prophesied:

"As Moses lifted up the snake in the wilderness, even so must the Son of Man be lifted up" (Jn 3:14).

51

Israel encountered several battles as kings came out to attack them on their way north, and Israel won them all. They took all the lands except Edom, Moab and Ammon, their relatives. The people of Edom were the descendents of Esau, Jacob's brother, and the people of Moab and Ammon were the descendents of the sons of Lot, Abraham's nephew.

The false prophet Balaam (Num 22-25)

Chapters 22-24 record the incident of the false prophet Balaam and king Balak of Moab. When Balak saw the victories of Israel, he was afraid and sent messengers with money to the prophet Balaam to pronounce a curse on Israel. Three times Balaam went to prophesy a curse on Israel, but Yahuah instead gave him words of blessing. The third one was a Messianic prophecy (Num 24:17-19).

Because Yahuah prevented Balaam from pronouncing a curse on Israel, Balaam told Balak what to do so that Yahuah would curse them. The book of Numbers doesn't give us this detail, but the book of Revelation does. He taught *"Israel to eat food offered to idols and to commit immorality"* (Rev 2:14). And so they did (Num 25:1-3).

Because of this, Yahuah sentenced Balaam to death. We will see this happen later.

So that the anger of Yahuah would be turned away from Israel, all the leaders of Israel involved in this idolatry and immorality were executed and hung in the sun, and then the other leaders were ordered to kill those under them who were joined to the god Baal Peor.

In the meantime, Yahuah sent a plague of death on Israel. The plague was stopped when Phinehas, son of the high priest Eleazar, killed a man of Israel and the Midian woman he was lying with by thrusting them both through with a spear.

And those who died in the plague were 24,000 (Num 25:9).

Because of what Phinehas did in Yahuah's zeal, so that Yahuah would not destroy all the children of Israel, Yahuah gave him and his descendants a covenant of an everlasting priesthood. This is a type of the bride.

Arrival across from the Promised Land (Num 27-31)

The 40 years of wandering in the wilderness now being up, Moses will die. Even though he was not permitted to enter the Promised Land because of striking the rock twice, Yahuah did let him see it from the top of Mount Nebo (Num 27:12-14).

Before dying, Moses ordered a new census, or numbering, of the new generation. This was of those still alive who were under 20 years old at the time of leaving Egypt, and all those born along the way. He also asked for a successor to be over the congregation. Yahuah appointed Joshua and had some of Moses' esteem put on him: *"so that all the congregation of the children of Israel obey him"* (Num 27:17-20).

Then, at the command of Yahuah, Moses took vengeance for Yahuah on Midian by ordering that they all be killed for what they did to Israel. But the army that went out killed only all the men, including Balaam, and took the women and children as captives. Yet it was the women who had enticed Israel into idolatry and immorality! So Moses ordered that all the women and all the male children be killed.

> *"But keep alive for yourselves all the female children who have not known a man by lying with a man"* (Num 31:18).

Israel was being prepared to cross over into the Promised Land and possess it. Moses described the boundaries of the land for the various tribes to possess, but they would have to drive out the inhabitants to gain the possession. In type, this is the person who is born again having to overcome his flesh nature and learn to live according to his newborn spirit nature.

Today, what Israel was told to do we would call genocide and would wonder at the "cruelty" of Yahuah to order that this be done. Keep in mind, though, that Yahuah is love and light and all that is righteous and good, and he alone is the owner of the earth and all the land on it. Those who occupy land do so only at the permission of Yahuah, and he can remove anyone and bring in anyone at his pleasure. And the reason for moving people about, with wars and conquering and "natural" disasters and plagues, is to gain as many people as possible who will love him with all their heart, soul, mind and strength and thus enter the eternal kingdom. This present earth is only temporary, and human life on it is only a probation period to discover those who have a bride's heart for Messiah. It is good to have this eternal perspective on history and current events.

In the case of the Canaanites, those who occupied the land, their wickedness had reached to the full measure and it was time for their removal, just as it was at the time of Noah, and so it will be during the plagues preceding Messiah's return. Among other things, they were involved in human sacrifices and burning babies alive. Sometimes Yahuah kills by natural disasters, such as the flood at the time of Noah. Billions of people died in that flood. Other times he has one nation make war on another nation to destroy it. Everything that happens is directed by Yahuah to achieve his ultimate purpose for creation, to make man in his likeness, while at the same time maintaining the free will of man.

By this time they had already conquered a large section of land on the east side of Jordan, and three tribes asked if they could occupy that land as their inheritance. Moses agreed, provided that their fighting men crossed over to help the others gain their inheritance, even as the others had helped them. Those three tribes were Gad, Reuben and half of the tribe of Manasseh.

Note that the tribe of Levi has no inheritance, and that Joseph has two portions through his sons Ephraim and Manasseh. The inheritance of the Levites was Yahuah himself. They were the priests on behalf of the others. So each tribe had to give cities within their own boundaries for the Levites to live in and open land around the cities for them to do their farming, for a total of 48 cities. Further, six of those 48 cities were to be cities of refuge, whereby if someone killed someone accidentally he could flee to it and be protected from being killed by a relative of the dead person, called "the avenger of blood." The priest in that city would determine whether the death was accidental or intentional. If not accidental, then the murderer would be put out of the city to be killed by "the avenger of blood."

5. Deuteronomy

THE TITLE "DEUTERONOMY" means "second law." It was the older generation that died in the wilderness that heard the law given at Mount Horeb. Now the new generation needed to hear it. They were on the east bank of the Jordan River across from the city of Jericho, and they were being prepared to cross over and enter the land. Almost everything in this book is a repeat of what already has been covered, both the laws and the events on the journey to the Promised Land. The new generation needed to know their history, and what would result from rebellion against Yahuah and his chosen leader (we have seen plenty of that), and what would result from obedience.

Although this is a "repeat" of history and laws, plus some added ones, there are a few things to look at. We begin with the greatest commandment of all.

The greatest commandment (Dt 6:4-5)

> *Hear, Israel: Yahuah our Elohim, Yahuah is one!* ⁵ *And you shall love Yahuah your Elohim with all your heart and with all your being and with all your might* (Dt 6:4-5).

The reason for driving out the inhabitants (Dt 9:3-6)

They also needed to know that it was not because of their righteousness, wisdom or strength that Yahuah was giving them the land and driving out the people before them. Indeed, they were a stiff-necked people. Rather, it is because of the wickedness of the people living there that he was driving them out, and also in order to establish his word that he swore to their fathers, to Abraham, Isaac and Jacob.

By the mouth of two or three witnesses (Dt 17:6)

> *At the mouth of two or three witnesses shall he that is to die be put to death. He is not put to death by the mouth of one witness* (Dt 17:6)..

This is a principle that goes beyond the death penalty. It is a principle for establishing truth in any situation. Yahushua referred to it himself when being accused (Jn 5:31-37). One application of this principle is signs, wonders, miracles and healings given in the name of Yahushua to confirm the message being spoken. The message is one witness, and the miracles are the second witness.

Laws regarding prophets (Dt 18)

Yahuah promised Moses he would raise up a prophet like him from among his brothers, a human like himself, who would always speak what Yahuah commanded him (Dt 18:15,18). This was a prophecy about Messiah, a human just like Moses.

Yahuah also said that a prophet who presumes to speak in his name saying anything Yahuah didn't command, or speaks in the name of other elohim, he is to be put to death. One way to know if a prophet who claims to be speaking for Yahuah is false is if what he has spoken doesn't come to pass (Dt 18:20-22).

Blessings and cursings (Dt 27-28)

In chapters 27 and 28 we have the blessings to be pronounced on Mount Gerizim and the cursings to be pronounced on Mount Ebal. The blessings will come as the result of obedience, and the cursings as the result of disobedience (Dt 28:1-2). The blessings are an automatic result of obedience. We don't make the blessings happen—Yahuah gives them. Although the blessings refer to the physical realm, they are types of blessings in the spiritual realm. The city is a type of the assembly, the field a type of the harvest field of souls, and the basket and kneading bowl a type of the word of Elohim.

And all peoples of the earth shall see that the name of Yahuah is called upon you, and they shall be afraid of you (Dt 28:10).

The cursings are the opposite of this, and go beyond to show what will happen to them as a nation because of their sin (Dt 28:15,20,34).

The death of Moses (Dt 33-34)

In chapter 33 Moses prophetically blesses each of the tribes, and chapter 34 describes the death of Moses. He was 120 years old when he died, eyes not dim nor his freshness gone.

And since then no prophet has arisen in Israel like Moses, whom Yahuah knew face to face, [11] for all the signs and wonders which Yahuah sent him to do in the land of Egypt before Pharaoh and before all his servants, and in all his land, [12] and for all that strong hand and in all the great fearsome deeds which Moses did before the eyes of all Israel (Dt 34:10-12).

We have now traveled from the beginning of creation, through the flood, and through the lives of the Patriarchs (Abraham, Isaac and Jacob) and Joseph. We have journeyed 40 years with Moses from Egypt to the Plain of Moab across from the Promised Land, and picked up the Torah (Law) and the Tent of Meeting (Tabernacle) on the way. We have seen the truth of the words:

> *The heart is deceitful above all things and desperately wicked.*
> *Who can understand it?* (Jer 17:9).

We have seen the blessings that come to those who obey Yahuah their Elohim from a heart of love, and the judgments that come to those who love themselves and rebel against their creator and against those whom he has appointed to be his spokesmen and leaders. We have examined how this history is a type of salvation, of our progress in maturity in the Master, and of the struggle between the flesh-man and the spirit-man. And we have seen the kind of attitude that is necessary to be a part of that company of believers called the bride of Messiah.

We now move on to the next stage, crossing the Jordan River and taking the land.

TWELVE HISTORICAL BOOKS

THE FIVE BOOKS OF THE TORAH (the Law, the five books of Moses) are the story of man from creation to when Israel is about to enter the Promised Land. It is a story filled with man's rebellion against Yahuah their Elohim and creator. The fifth book ended with the curse that Israel would be evicted from the land if they didn't follow the Torah.

The twelve Historical Books tell of the twelve tribes of Israel conquering the land, getting a king, being united into a nation, being divided into two nations, being evicted from the land, and a remnant returning to the land. As with the five books of the Torah, it is a story filled with man's rebellion against Yahuah their Elohim and creator, and is a type of the assembly's rebellion in its history.

We begin with the successor of Moses leading the people across the Jordan River and conquering much of the Promised Land.

1. Joshua

T HE NAME JOSHUA in Hebrew is Yahushua, the same as for Jesus. Tradition spells them differently in English to show they are different people. This "Survey" does the same so as to avoid confusion.

The Book of Joshua is divided into three sections. Chapters 1-12 give the conquest of the land. Chapters 13-22 give the division of the land among the tribes as instructed by Moses. And chapters 23 and 24 give the farewell address and death of Joshua. In this survey we skip over section 2, the division of the land.

In the first few verses of this book Yahuah instructs Joshua to cross the Jordan and lead the people into the land. All the land they walk on is theirs, from the wilderness in the south to Lebanon in the north, and from the Jordan to the Great Sea (Mediterranean).

> *"No man is going to stand before you all the days of your life. As I was with Moses, so I am with you. I will not fail you nor forsake you. ⁶ Be strong and courageous, for you shall divide the land for an inheritance for this people which I swore to their fathers to give them"* (Jos 1:5-6).

Two spies sent and the promise to Rahab (Jos 2)

Joshua sent two men to spy out the land, and when they came to the house of Rahab in Jericho (which was on the city's outer wall) they slept there (Jos 2:1). Rahab is a type of the bride yet in the world. She hid the spies from the king of Jericho, and asked that she and her family be saved alive when Israel takes the city. They agreed, provided that when the time comes she will tie a scarlet cord in the window, the one through which they will escape out of the city (Jos 2:17-18). In type, scarlet, the color of the cord, represents the blood of Yahushua Messiah who died to save us from our sins.

When the spies returned they reported to Joshua:

> *"Truly Yahuah has given all the land into our hands, and also, all the inhabitants of the land have become disheartened because of us"* (Jos 2:24).

What a different report from the report of 10 of the 12 spies sent out by Moses!

Israel crosses the Jordan (Jos 3-4)

They crossed the Jordan during the time of harvest, a time when the river overflows all its banks and not a good time to the natural mind. But the priests who were carrying the Box of the Covenant before the people, when their feet touched the edge of the water, an invisible dam stopped the river so that it piled upstream as far as the city of Adam, and the people passed over opposite Jericho on dry ground. And the priests carrying the Box stood in the middle of the Jordan until all had passed over (Jos 3:14-17). This is a type of Messiah, by his death, providing forgiveness for sin for all mankind, going back to Adam.

After crossing over, as a memorial of what Yahuah had done for them, they took 12 stones, one for each tribe, from the middle of the river, and placed them at Gilgal, the place where they camped (Jos 4:1-13).

> *On that day Yahuah exalted Joshua in the sight of all Israel so that they respected him, just as they had respected Moses all the days of his life* (Jos 4:14).

When the rulers of the Amorites and the Canaanites heard about this miracle, they became disheartened, *"and there was no spirit in them any longer because of the children of Israel"* (Jos 5:1).

Even though all the inhabitants heard of this miracle and could clearly see that Yahuah, the Elohim of Israel, was more powerful than any of their elohim (gods, mighty ones), they did not repent and convert to Yahuah as Rahab had. They loved their wickedness.

Israel circumcised at Gilgal (Jos 5)

None of those born during the 40 years of wilderness travel had been circumcised according to the covenant with Abraham. So at Gilgal where they camped after crossing the Jordan they did it, and stayed there until they were healed. And Yahuah said to Joshua, *"This day I have rolled away the reproach of Egypt from you"* (Jos 5:9). Gilgal means rolled away.

They crossed over on the tenth day of the first month. This was the same day when in Egypt they selected a lamb which would be offered on the fourteenth of the month for Passover. This was the fortieth year since that event. And on the fourteenth of the month they performed the Passover. The morning after the Passover they ate unleavened bread and roasted grain made from the stored grain of the land, that which the inhabitants had stored up after the barley harvest. The following day the manna stopped (Jos 5:10-12). They had been eating it for forty years, but no more, for all the harvest of the inhabitants was now theirs, given to them by Yahuah their Elohim.

This was not stealing. Everything—land, produce and animals—belongs to Yahuah, and he gives them to whomever he wills. It is he who created vegetation and animals with life in them. It is he who brings the rain and sunshine and enables them to grow and become food for man whom he created. The resident nations had brought their wickedness to the full, and they no longer had a right to the blessings of the land, cities and harvest. Yahuah was evicting them.

Israel conquers Jericho (Jos 6)

Jericho was the first city on the west side of the Jordan to be captured, and in a most unusual way. The men of battle walked around the city once a day for six days. They were told not to speak any word during this time. With them were seven priests blowing shophars (rams' horns) and carrying the Box of the Covenant. On the seventh day they did this seven times. This seventh time, however, when the priests blew the shophars, they all shouted, the walls fell down flat, and the people went into the city to capture it (Jos 6:16-20). Archeology has revealed that Jericho had three walls, one inside the other, and that all the walls had fallen outward, making it easy for Israel to enter from all sides.

The city had been "put under the ban." That means the city was to be burned to the ground, everything was to be destroyed, and everyone was to be killed, man, woman and child, except Rahab and her family. Also, they were to take no loot for themselves. The exceptions were to bring out Rahab and her relatives, and to keep the silver and gold and vessels of bronze and of iron for the treasury of the house of Yahuah (Jos 6:23-24).

Ai defeats Israel, Achan's sin, Israel defeats Ai (Jos 7; 8:1-29)

After conquering Jericho, Israel next attempted to take Ai (ah-EE).

They thought it would be easy, but they failed, about 36 of them being killed as they ran from the Ai warriors. They failed because Yahuah was not with them, and this was because Achan , one of their own, had taken from Jericho a Babylonian garment, some silver, and a wedge of gold, and hidden them in his tent, thereby breaking the command to destroy everyone and everything in that city. The sentence against him was that he experience the judgment against Jericho; namely, that he with his family and livestock and all that he owned be destroyed, except the gold and silver. In this way Yahuah's anger was appeased (Jos 7:24-26).

Then Yahuah gave Joshua a battle plan whereby they defeated Ai. This time they were allowed to take plunder for themselves, but they were to burn the city to the ground.

Blessings at Gerizim and Cursings at Ebal (Jos 8:30-38)

After Israel defeated Ai, they went to Mount Gerizim and Mount Ebal and pronounced the blessings and cursings as Moses had directed them—blessings if they obeyed, and cursings if they didn't obey. Spiritually, these blessings and cursings apply to us believers.

Israel deceived by Gibeon (Jos 9)

The other cities, having heard what happened to Jericho and Ai, gathered together to fight Israel, hoping that a larger army would be successful. Yahuah had commanded Israel to destroy all the inhabitants, but Gibeon tricked Israel into making a treaty by pretending to be from a land far away instead of being near. Instead of asking Yahuah for wisdom, they believed Gibeon and made a peace treaty with them (Jos 9:14-15). When Joshua found out they had been deceived, he made them slaves to be woodcutters and drawers of water for the House of Elohim (Jos 9:23-25).

Israel conquers the kings, and the sun stands still (Jos 10-11)

Because Gibeon had made peace with Israel, five kings joined together to destroy Gibeon. Gibeon appealed to Joshua, and Israel defeated the five kings with the help of Yahuah. Yahuah threw the armies of the five kings into confusion and threw down large hailstones from the sky. Further, in order to have enough daylight to finish slaying the enemy, Joshua prayed to Yahuah for the sun to stand still, and Yahuah gave him the longer day (Jos 10:1-14).

The rest of these two chapters relates the conquering of the southern city states and then the northern city states. Kings would join together to fight Israel, and be defeated. However, not all the land was taken, for Yahuah left some in the land to test Israel.

Distribution of the land and warnings (Jos 13-24)

These chapters relate the distribution of the land to the various tribes according to their boundaries. This included sending Reuben, Gad and the half tribe of Manasseh back to their land east of Jordan. But, as was mentioned, not all the land was taken. It was now up to each tribe to finish taking the land allotted to them.

Then Joshua gave them the same warning that Moses had given regarding the result of obedience to Yahuah and the result of disobedience. Obedience would bring blessing; disobedience would bring failure to conquer the rest of the land, and eventually they would be evicted from the land.

In type, when we get born again, a big spiritual victory happens in our lives. We have moved from the kingdom of darkness into the kingdom of light. We have chosen to leave the way of Satan (a way of selfishness and pride) and have chosen to live the way of Messiah (a way of selflessness and humility). We now have a reborn spirit. So this is a very big victory. But much of the flesh nature is still with us. We have habit patterns of the flesh that we still love. These are areas of "land" in our lives still to be conquered. And this fight against the "flesh" will continue until we die. It is a fight to love Yahuah our Elohim with all our heart, soul, mind and strength. It is a fight to love him and others more than ourselves. Yahushua Messiah said we are to enter through the narrow gate that leads to life, but few find it. The wide gate leads to destruction, and many enter through it (Mt 7:13-14).

But he has made all the provision necessary to find the small gate and narrow road. All those who keep pursuing him will indeed find it, for he is with us always, to the end of the age (Mt 28:18).

2. Judges

IN THE BEGINNING of the book of Judges the various tribes help one another to continue conquering the land that was given to them. But they had mixed success so that always Canaanites were still living among them. When the children of Israel were stronger, they made the Canaanites slaves instead of destroying them and their idolatry from the land. This displeased Yahuah, so he would no longer drive them out, but rather that they would become thorns in their sides and their elohim (gods) would be a snare to them (Jdg 2:1-3). This is the result of compromise with the world and giving up on getting sin out of your life.

During the life of Joshua and during the lives of the elders who outlived Joshua, Israel served Yahuah, for they had seen the miracles that brought them into the land. But when the last of the elders died, the new generation that arose and which had not seen the miracles did evil in the eyes of Yahuah, taking on the customs and religion of the people and playing the harlot with their elohim (gods).

As a result, Yahuah let them be conquered by the pagans. When the distress of Israel became too great, Israel cried out to Yahuah for help, and he would have pity on them and send them deliverers (judges) to rescue them. But when the deliverer died, they would go back to their idolatry, and Yahuah would punish them again by letting the pagans conquer them again. And again they would cry to Yahuah, and in his mercy would send another deliverer. And when that deliverer died they would go back to idolatry again. And so it was throughout this period, over and over.

And the anger of Yahuah burned against Israel, and he said, "Because this nation has transgressed my covenant that I commanded their fathers and has not listened to my voice, I also shall no longer drive out before them any of the nations which Joshua left when he died, in order to test Israel by them, whether they would keep the way of Yahuah, to walk in them as their fathers kept them, or not" (Jdg 2:20-22).

In this survey we will look briefly at some of the judges.

Othniel (Jdg 3:7-11)

Othniel was the first judge (Jdg 3:7-11). It is said of him:

And the spirit of Yahuah came upon him and he judged Israel and went out to battle, ... and the land had rest for forty years. And Othniel ... died. The sons of Israel again did evil in the sight of Yahuah. ... And they served Eglon the king of Moab eighteen years (Jdg 3:10-12,14).

Ehud and Shamgar (Jdg 3:15-31)

Ehud was the second judge. He was left-handed. He tricked king Eglon of Moab into being alone with him, and thrust him through with his sword (Jdg 3:21-22). Then Ehud escaped and called Israel to join him in defeating Moab. And the land had rest for 80 years.

Shamgar, the third judge, was known for smiting 600 men of the Philistines with an ox goad. He lived during the time of Ehud.

Deborah and Barak (Jdg 4-5)

After 20 years of being oppressed by Jabin the king of Canaan, Yahuah raised up Deborah, a prophetess, and Barak. Deborah told Barak that Yahuah wanted him to fight Sisera, Jabin's commander. Barak agreed to go, but only if Deborah went with him. Barak gathered an army of 10,000 men to go against Sisera who had 900 chariots of iron plus numerous warriors. In the ensuing battle Yahuah destroyed Sisera's army, and Sisera leaped from his chariot and fled away on foot to the tent of Jael. She gave him some milk and covered him with a blanket. When he fell asleep, she drove a tent peg through his head into the ground (Jdg 4:21).

And the land had rest forty years (Jdg 5:31).

Gideon and sons (Jdg 6-9)

And the sons of Israel did evil in the eyes of Yahuah, and Yahuah gave them into the hand of Midian for seven years (Jdg 6:1).

The situation of Israel was such that they had to hide in the mountains and caves, and they could not openly do any harvesting of crops, and all their animals were taken. Eventually, when it got bad enough, they cried out to Yahuah for help. In answer to their prayer, the messenger (angel) of Yahuah appeared to Gideon and called him to be the leader to smite Midian.

Gideon was given several signs to confirm that it was indeed Yahuah who had called him. In the first sign, Gideon brought an offering of meat and unleavened bread and lay them on a rock and poured out broth on it. The messenger of Yahuah touched the meat and bread with the end of his staff, and fire went up out of the rock and consumed the food (Jdg 6:19-23).

That same night Yahuah told him to destroy the altar of Baal that his father had along with the Asherah beside it, then to build an altar to Yahuah on top of the rock, put the wood of the image on it, and make a burnt offering using one of his father's bulls (Jdg 6:25-26).

This shows that the people hadn't repented, even though they had called out to Yahuah for help, for they were still bowing to Baal. In type, this is Babylon in the assembly, yet the members are still wanting Elohim to help them. But Yahuah has his leaders who will tear down the false doctrines and practices in the assembly, not literally, but through teaching confirmed with signs and wonders, just as Yahushua Messiah did with the Jews.

Gideon, with the help of his servants, did it secretly at night. In the morning when the men of the city saw what had happened, they wanted to kill Gideon. But his father, Joash, said to them that if Baal is a god let him plead for himself. On that day they called him Jerubbaal (Baal will contend).

Then Midian and Amalek and the people of the East gathered in the Valley of Jezreel together to fight Israel.

Then the spirit of Yahuah came upon Gideon, and he blew the shophar, and [many people from various tribes] gathered behind him (Jdg 6:34).

This is a type of the bride calling out to the bride, and the bride responding.

Throughout Israel's history many battles were fought in the Valley of Jezreel. In the book of Revelation this valley is called Armageddon, where the nations of the world gather together to come against Jerusalem.

Gideon is still unsure about going against such a powerful army that faced him, so he asked Yahuah for two more signs, using a fleece of wool. For the first sign he placed the fleece on the ground overnight and asked that only the fleece have dew in the morning and the ground be dry. Yahuah did as he asked. For the second sign, just to be sure, he asked for it to be the other way around, that the ground be wet with dew but not the fleece. Again, Yahuah did as he asked.

When the Father is asking you to do something that is dangerous, it is good to get confirmation from him that it is truly the Father that is doing the asking and not something from your own mind or from a fallen spirit. Not only was Gideon risking his own life, but the lives of thousands of others as well.

The people who gathered to Gideon were 32,000. Yahuah wanted that number smaller lest the people think it was their own might that conquered the enemy. So he had all those who were afraid to go back home. 22,000 left, leaving 10,000. That was still too many, so Yahuah tested them by having them drink from a stream. Yahuah told Gideon to separate those who knelt to drink from those who drank from their hands. Those who knelt were sent home and the remaining were chosen. By this group, 300 men of battle, Yahuah would give Midian into their hand.

It should be noted that those who knelt to drink were in a vulnerable position if an enemy attacked. This shows they were not alert to danger, and that fighting to win was not on their minds. That is why they were disqualified to be among the chosen. In contrast, those who scooped up water with their hands *"and lapped like a dog"* were still upright, had their hands on their swords, and were ready to fight at a moment's notice. This is why they were chosen.

In type, we have the lazy believer who thinks more of himself than the kingdom, and we have the industrious, kingdom-minded believer whose mind is always on rescuing souls from the enemy to bring them into the kingdom.

The enemy were in the valley, and Gideon with his 300 men were on the hill above. He divided them into three groups, and gave to each of the men a shophar (ram's horn), an empty clay jar, and a lit torch in each jar. (Light could not shine through the clay.) When they came to the edge of the camp of the enemy, they all broke their clay jars, held their torches in one hand, blew on their shophars and shouted, *"For*

Yahuah and for Gideon!" Then all the enemy fled leaving their belongings behind, for they thought that each torch and shophar sound was a whole division of Israel's army (Jdg 7:16-22).

As a result of this great victory, the men of Israel wanted Gideon to rule over them, and his son, and his son's son. But Gideon refused, saying Yahuah is the ruler. But he did something that became a snare to Israel. From their plunder he made a shoulder garment, like a priest's ephod, and set it up in Ophrah, his city (Jdg 8:22-27a).

> *And all Israel prostituted themselves to it there* (spiritually). *And it became a snare to Gideon and to his family. ... And the land had rest for forty years in the days of Gideon. ... And it came to be, when Gideon was dead, that the children of Israel again went prostituting after the Baals, and made Baal-Berith their mighty one* (Jdg 8:27-28,33).

Chapter 9 relates a sad story regarding Gideon's sons. He had 70 sons because of his many wives and concubines. One son, Abimelek, plotted to become king and killed all his brothers, except one who hid. Then a civil war began in which many died, and eventually Abimelek himself was mortally wounded when a woman threw a millstone on his head from a tower he was attacking. Not wanting it said that a woman killed him, he had a servant kill him with a sword.

Jephthah (Jdg 11)

We skip over a few judges to Jephthah. He had been exiled from Gilead by his brothers because his mother was a prostitute and they didn't want him to share in the inheritance. While in exile he proved himself to be an able leader and warrior. So when Ammon fought against Israel, the elders of Gilead asked Jephthah to come back. Jephthah agreed on the condition that if Yahuah gave him victory over Ammon, that the elders would accept him as their leader, and the elders agreed.

Before going to battle, however, Jephthah made a foolish vow to Yahuah, that if he gave Ammon into his hands, whatever first comes out of the door of his house to meet him would belong to Yahuah and be offered up as a burnt offering (Jdg 11:30-31). He did win, but when he came home it was his daughter that came out to meet him.

This grieved him greatly because of his vow, a vow which he felt bound to keep. And his daughter agreed that the vow should be kept, and had permission to be alone for two months to wander on the mountains and bewail her maidenhood, she with her friends. After the two months she returned home:

> *And he did to her as he had vowed, and she knew no man* (Jdg 11:39).

Scholars debate as to whether she was actually slain as a burnt offering, or she only remained unmarried.

Samson (Jdg 13-16)

We skip over a few more judges and come to Samson. Because of their sin, Yahuah had given Israel into the hand of the Philistines for 40 years. A man named Manoah of the tribe of Dan had a wife who was barren. (This is similar in type to Rachael and Sarah.) A messenger of Yahuah appeared to the wife and told her she would have a son. She was to name him Samson, and his hair was never to be cut, nor was he to drink wine or strong drink or eat any (ceremonially) unclean food:

> *"For the youth is a Nazirite to Elohim from the womb on. And he shall begin to save Israel out of the hand of the Philistines"* (Jdg 13:5).

There are many strange details of his life, the most of which resulted because of his great strength. In none of these activities, however, was he a leader of an army to fight the Philistines. Rather, Yahuah set up circumstances in which Samson slew many Philistines all by himself.

Samson's first episode included a riddle which he told the Philistines in Timnah at a feast he held, for he had chosen a wife from there. They would give him 30 linen garments and 30 changes of garments if they couldn't solve it in the seven days of the feast, and vice versa. The riddle was based on something Samson had done earlier. He had killed a lion with his bare hands, and later when he saw the carcass it had a swarm of bees and honey in it, and he ate the honey. The riddle was:

> *"Out of the eater came forth food,*
> *And out of the strong came forth sweetness"* (Jdg 14:14).

When they couldn't solve the riddle they threatened Samson's wife to get the answer, which she did after seven days of much pleading and weeping. On the seventh day of the feast the men gave Samson the answer:

> *"What is sweeter than honey?*
>> *And what is stronger than a lion?"* (Jdg 14:18).

Samson replied:

> *"If you had not plowed with my heifer,*
>> *You would not have solved my riddle!"* (Jdg 14:18).

Then the spirit of Yahuah came on him mightily, and he killed 30 men in another town of the Philistines to get the garments. He went back to his father's house, and his wife was given to another man (Jdg 14:14-20).

Later, when Samson went to get his wife, her father told him he had given her to another. In retaliation, Sampson caught 300 foxes and turned them tail to tail, tied torches between each pair of tails, set the torches on fire, and sent them out into the standing grain of the Philistines, and burned up the standing grain, the shocks, and even the vineyards and olive trees. When the Philistines learned why Samson had done this, they went up and burned to death Samson's wife and her father (Jdg 15:4-8).

This incident of the riddle and what followed is given in detail for two reasons. One, it is a good example of the kind of ministry Samson had as a judge. Two, it is a good example of how riddles and poetry were used in their culture. It was common for them to speak in riddles and in proverbs. This is somewhat an introduction to what we will see later when we get to the poetry books.

In another daring act, Samson killed a thousand men with *"a fresh jawbone of a donkey"* (Jdg 15:15).

The most familiar story of Samson is his relationship with a prostitute named Delilah, whom he loved. The princes of the Philistines offered much money to Delilah to discover the secret of Samson's strength and thereby overpower and humble him. She begged Samson for the secret, for if he truly loved her he would tell her. (This has a similarity to what Samson's wife did, as we saw earlier.) Philistines were hiding in her room, waiting for the answer so they could bind him. Eventually, after giving a few false reasons, he told the truth. It was his hair. If it were shaved off he would lose his strength.

Samson fell asleep on her knees, and the men in hiding shaved off the seven locks of his head. His strength left him, and he didn't know that Yahuah had turned aside from him. They bound him with bronze shackles, put out his eyes, and put him in prison as a grinder, but his hair began to grow again (Jdg 16:19-22).

Later, when the Philistines had a big party to honor Dagon their god and thank Dagon for delivering their enemy Samson to them, they called for Samson to come so they could mock him for entertainment. There were about 3,000 men and women on the roof looking on. Samson prayed to Yahuah for strength to avenge himself for his two eyes. With his hands on the two center columns that supported the house:

> *He bowed himself mightily, and the house fell on the princes and all the people in it. And the dead that he killed at his death were more than he had killed in his life* (Jdg 16:30).

In type, this is the bride of Messiah male son ministry in the last days dealing a death blow to the one world antichrist government before the rapture. There is much more typology in Samson's life; this has been a sampling.

Gross sin in Israel (Jdg 17-21).

These chapters are a collection of two stories of gross immorality that happened some time during the early years of the period of the Judges. The first is about the tribe of Dan seeking their inheritance and the idolatry of a man named Micah.

The second is about a Levite whose concubine was killed by men of the tribe of Benjamin in the city of Gibeah. The Levite had stopped there on his way home. The men wanted to sodomize the Levite, but the Levite gave them his concubine instead, and they raped her to death. When the Levite got home with his dead concubine, he cut her body into twelve pieces and sent the pieces throughout Israel so they would know what the Benjamites of Gibeah had done.

The other tribes of Israel gathered against the city because of this wickedness, wanting the city to surrender the men who had done this so they could kill them *"and put away evil from Israel."* Instead of agreeing, men from the other cities of Benjamin joined those of Gibeah to fight the other tribes of Israel (Jdg 20:11-14).

The men of Benjamin with 26,700 men came against the men of Israel who were 400,000 men. On the first day of the battle, 22,000 of Israel died. On the second day, 18,000 more of Israel died. On the third day, with the help of Yahuah, Israel killed all the men of Benjamin, except for 600 who had fled to a fortress. Then Israel turned back and burned all the cities of Benjamin and killed all their men and beasts (Jdg 20:17-48).

The story continues with how 600 wives were found for the 600 men of Benjamin, so that Benjamin would not cease to be a tribe among them (Jdg 21). This ends the sad saga of the book of Judges.

In those days there was no king in Israel—everyone did what was right in his own eyes (Jdg 17:6; 21:25)..

3. Ruth

THE STORY OF RUTH takes place during the time of the Judges. It is the story of how Ruth, a woman of Moab and therefore a gentile, became the wife of Boaz, a man of Israel, and thus be listed as one of the ancestors of Yahushua Messiah. It is an amazing story and full of typology for believers in Yahushua. Boaz is a type of Messiah, Naomi is a type of the assembly of Messiah, and Ruth is a type of the gentile assembly of Messiah having the heart of the bride and thus maturing from conversion to becoming the bride.

The story begins with a famine in Bethlehem of Judah (in type, famine for the word of Elohim in the assembly). Because of the famine, a man named Elimelech took his wife Naomi and his two sons to Moab (east of the Jordan River) to make a living (in type, going to the world for comfort rather than trusting Elohim). While there Elimelech died (in type, lost his salvation), Naomi's two sons took Moabite wives named Orpah and Ruth, and they lived there for about ten years (a type of completeness in this world). Then the two sons died and the widow Naomi had two widowed daughters-in-law. When Naomi heard that Yahuah had ended the famine in Bethlehem (in type, Yahuah had brought revival to the assembly), she decided to go back to her home there. When Orpah and Ruth started going with her, she told them to go back and not follow. But Ruth refused to turn back, saying:

> *"Do not urge me to leave you or to go back from following after you. For wherever you go, I go; and wherever you stop over, I will stop over. Your people are my people and your Elohim is my Elohim. Where you die, I die, and there I shall be buried."* (Ruth 1:16-17).

We see here a full conversion of Ruth from the religion of Moab to Yahuah, the true Elohim.

When Naomi and Ruth arrived in Bethlehem they were destitute. They had Naomi's former house, but no land, money or income. But Naomi did have a wealthy relative on her husband's side, a man named Boaz. Yahuah arranged for Ruth and Boaz to meet in this way. To get food for herself and Naomi, Ruth went into a field to do gleaning behind the reapers, and it so happened that the field she went to belonged to Boaz. (Gleaning is gathering grain or other produce left behind in a field after harvest) Upon inquiry Boaz found out all about Ruth, how she came to be there, how industrious she was in gleaning, and his relationship to her through Naomi. So he gave her favor by arranging for her to have much harvest from the gleaning.

> The corners of fields were not to be reaped, and the sheaf accidentally left behind was not to be fetched away, according to the law of Moses (Lev 19:9; 23:22; Deut 24:21). They were to be left for the poor to glean. Similar laws were given regarding vineyards and oliveyards. (Easton's Bible Dictionary)

Ruth gleaned through both the barley harvest (a type of Passover, which is a type of born again) and the wheat harvest (a type of Pentecost, which is a type of immersion in the spirit) (Ruth 2:23).

When Naomi learned that Ruth was gleaning in the field belonging to Boaz and that Boaz was giving her favor, she told Ruth what to do to get Boaz to marry her (by following local customs). In type, this is the assembly teaching the members how to become the bride of Messiah. The custom had to do with the right of a kinsman redeemer.

> Kinsman — Heb. *goel*, [go-AIL] from a root meaning to redeem. The *goel* among the Hebrews was the nearest male blood relation alive. Certain important obligations devolved upon him toward his next of kin. (1.) If anyone from poverty was unable to redeem his inheritance, it was the duty of the kinsman to redeem it (Lev

25:25,28; Ruth 3:9,12). ...

God is the *Goel* of his people because he redeems them (Ex 6:6; Isa 43:1; 41:14; 44:6,22; 48:20; Ps 103:4; Job 19:25, etc.).

(Easton's Bible Dictionary)

When Ruth let Boaz know that she was willing to be his wife on the basis of his being a redeemer, Boaz agreed, but said there was a redeemer nearer than he (Ruth 3:10-12). So the next morning he spoke to the other redeemer about redeeming the land, but also that if he did so he must also take Ruth, a woman of Moab, as his wife to raise up the name of the dead on his inheritance (Ruth 4:5). Because of this condition, the other redeemer gave up his right.

It was not an obligation by law for a redeemer to marry Ruth, even if he redeemed the land, since neither of the redeemers were full brothers of Naomi's deceased husband. (This is called the levirate law.) But rather it was a right which could be declined. Evidently, however, it was the custom at the time of Ruth that the one who redeemed the land also had an obligation to marry the widow.

Boaz then redeemed the land and took Ruth as his wife and the child born to them became the great-grandfather of King David.

4. First Samuel

THE BOOK OF FIRST SAMUEL is a transition from Judges to Kings, for Samuel was a judge (and prophet) who anointed the first two kings of Israel, Saul and David.

Samuel born and becomes a prophet (1Sa 1-2)

The book begins with a situation similar to that of Jacob who had two wives, one fruitful and the other barren. Elkanah of the tribe of Ephraim had two wives: Hannah the cherished one who was barren, and Peninnah who had children. In prayer to Yahuah, Hannah vowed that if she were granted a male child, then she would give him to Yahuah all his life and his hair would never be cut off. Yahuah granted her request, and she bore Samuel. The name means "asked of or heard of Elohim." At this time the Tent (Tabernacle) with the Box (Ark) of the Covenant was at Shiloh. It was moved there from Gilgal after Joshua completed his conquest.

When Samuel was weaned, which would be about three years old according to their custom, Hannah *"loaned him to Yahuah,"* and Samuel served before Eli the priest. Eli was a righteous man, but his two sons, Hophni and Phinehas, were wicked, taking from the offerings of the people whatever they wanted without regard to the Law. And Eli their father did not rebuke them.

When Eli was old and almost blind, Yahuah told Samuel that he was going to judge Eli. When Samuel grew up, all Israel acknowledged him to be a prophet (1Sa 3:13, 18-21).

The Box of Elohim captured and returned (1Sa 3-6)

When Israel went out to battle against the Philistines, the Philistines killed about 4,000 of them (1Sa 4:2). The elders of Israel thought that if they sent the Box of Elohim out in the battle Yahuah would be with them and they would win. But they were wrong. About 30,000 foot soldiers of Israel fell, the Box of Elohim was captured, and the two sons of Eli, Hophni and Phinehas, died (1Sa 4:10-11). When the news was brought to Eli, he also died, having ruled Israel for forty years.

> In Hebrew "Box" is a different word from "Ark." "Box" is *'aron* (aw-ROAN). It means a box or chest, something you use to put objects in. "Ark" is *tebah* (tay-BAH), and means a container that floats, such as Noah's ark and the floating basket in which Moses was placed.

The Philistines brought the Box of Elohim into the house of Dagon (the fish god) in Ashdod, and in the morning they saw Dagon fallen on its face on the ground before the Box of Yahuah. They put Dagon in its place again, but the next morning not only had Dagan fallen on its face before the Box, its head and both the palms of its hands were broken off. Further, the hand of Yahuah was heavy on the people of Ashdod, putting tumors on them (1Sa 5:3-7).

So they of Ashdod sent the Box to Gath, and then to Ekron. And in each Philistine city where the Box was kept, Yahuah brought deadly destruction, killing many and smiting those who didn't die with tumors. So the Philistines returned the Box to Israel by putting the Box with gifts on a wagon and having two milk cows (separated from their calves) pull it to Bethshemesh.

The men of Bethshemesh rejoiced to see the Box, but when they looked into the Box, Yahuah killed 70 of the men. So, being afraid to keep the Box, they sent to the people of Kiriathjearim to come and get it. When they came, they took it to the house of Abinadab in their city, where it stayed for 20 years.

Samuel calls to repentance and Philistines attack (1Sa 7)

Samuel called Israel to put away their idols and to prepare their hearts for Yahuah and serve only him, so that he may deliver them from the Philistines. He called all Israel to gather to Mizpah and he would pray for them. So Israel gathered there, fasted and repented. When the Philistines heard of their gathering, they came up against Israel, and Israel was afraid. When Samuel offered up the burnt offering, Yahuah thundered such a great noise that the Philistines were smitten before Israel, and Israel took back all the cities that the Philistines had taken from them. Also, there was peace between Israel and the Amorites.

Saul becomes king (1Sa 8-12)

When Samuel became old he made his sons rulers over Israel. Because his sons were wicked, the elders of Israel asked him to appoint a king to rule over them like all the nations (1Sa 8:3-5).

When Samuel asked Yahuah about it, Yahuah told him:

> *"They have not rejected you, but have rejected me from ruling over them"* (1Sa 8:7).

He reminded Samuel that this isn't new, for ever since he brought them out of Egypt they have always been forsaking him and serving other elohim. Then he told Samuel to do as they asked, but to warn them of the dangers of having a king (1Sa 8:7-9).

Samuel told the elders what Yahuah said and all the hardship that a king would impose on them, making them virtual slaves, so that they would cry to Yahuah for help, but Yahuah wouldn't listen to them when that time would come. Despite the warning, they still wanted a king to rule them and go out before them and fight their battles (1Sa 8:19-20).

Up to this time Israel was not a united nation, but rather a scattering of tribes with priests among their cities. They were supposed to be obeying Yahuah, living righteously, and destroying the native nations and their idolatry. If they did this, then Yahuah would give them peace and abundance (the blessings pronounced on Mount Gerizim) and they wouldn't need a king. But they didn't do this, so they didn't have abundance and they were constantly being oppressed by the nations (the cursings pronounced on Mount Ebal). That is why they wanted a king; they wanted to be like the pagan nations.

So Yahuah led Samuel in finding for them a king, and that man was Saul. Saul's first test as king was a battle against Ammon who had come against Israel. Under the leadership of Saul, Israel won (1Sa 11).

Saul's sin by offering burnt offerings (1Sa 13)

The Philistines had gathered to fight Israel with such a large force that the men of Israel were terrified and hid in caves and such, and some even left the territory. In the meantime, Saul was at Gilgal waiting for Samuel to show up to offer a burnt offering, and as he was waiting his army was scattering from him. Finally Saul decided he couldn't wait any longer, so offered the burnt offering. Just as he finished doing so, Samuel arrived. Samuel scolded him, that he had no authority to offer the burnt offering, and as a result of his disobedience his kingship would not stand and Yahuah would seek for himself a man after his own heart (1Sa 13:8-14). That man would be David, great-grandson of Boaz and Ruth.

Saul's foolish vow not to eat during battle (1Sa 14)

Soon after this Jonathan, Saul's son, and Jonathan's armor bearer attacked a Philistine outpost, and the result of this was that the whole army of Saul, including those who had scattered from him, defeated the Philistines. But Saul foolishly had placed his army under an oath that no one was to eat any food until the evening, and whoever did would be executed. Because of this vow, the army was losing strength to continue pursuing the Philistines. But Jonathan, not having heard the vow, ate some honey on the way and it gave him strength to fight harder. When Saul learned what his son had done, he wanted to kill him because of the vow. But the people persuaded Saul not to kill him, because he was the one who worked the great deliverance in Israel.

All the days of Saul there was fierce fighting against the Philistines, and when Saul saw any mighty or brave man, he took him for himself (1Sa 14:45-46, 52).

Saul fails to completely destroy Amalek (1Sa 15)

We saw earlier that Amalek, without provocation, came and fought with Israel in Rephidim, and that Israel won the battle by Aaron and Hur helping to hold Moses' hand up (Ex 17:8-16). Later, Moses told Israel that when they possessed their inheritance in the promised land that they were to blot out the remembrance of Amalek (Dt 25:19). So Saul was given the task of fulfilling this command by destroying all of Amalek, all humans of every age and sex and all animals (1Sa 15:1-3). But he failed to do it completely. He spared Agag the king and the best of the animals (1Sa 15:9).

When Samuel confronted Saul on his failure to fulfill all the command of Yahuah, Saul made excuses. In response Samuel said:

> *"Does Yahuah delight in burnt offerings and slaughterings*
> *As in obeying the voice of Yahuah?*
> *Look, to obey is better than an offering,*
> *To listen is better than the fat of rams.*
> *"For rebellion is as the sin of divination,*
> *And stubbornness is as wickedness and idolatry.*
> *Because you have rejected the word of Yahuah,*
> *He also rejects you as king"* (1Sa 15:22-23).

Then Samuel cut Agag in pieces before Yahuah in Gilgal, and Samuel never saw Saul again (1Sa 15:33-35).

David anointed and serves Saul (1Sa 16-17)

At this point David enters the scene. Samuel anointed David to be king, although David had many trials to go through before he would become king. The spirit of Yahuah came upon him from that day forward, and the spirit of Yahuah turned away from Saul, and an evil spirit from Yahuah troubled him (1Sa 16:13-14).

David's first encounter with Saul was when he was called to Saul's court. He became one of Saul's armor-bearers, and also refreshed Saul by playing his lyre when Saul was being troubled by the evil spirit (probably a spirit of depression).

David's second encounter with Saul was the occasion of his defeating Goliath *"with a sling and a stone,"* then cutting off Goliath's head with Goliath's own sword (1Sa 17:50-51). As a result, Saul set him over the men of battle. But when David would return from battle and the women sang, *"Saul killed his thousands, and David his ten-thousands"* (1Sa 18:7), Saul became jealous and threw a spear at him to kill him. The hatred in Saul continued to grow until finally David left. But Jonathan, Saul's son, supported David (1Sa 20:42).

David pursued by Saul (1Sa 21-30)

These chapters record David's wanderings while Saul is hunting him with his army to kill him. Here are a few highlights of this period.

At Nob (rhymes with robe) the priest gave David and his young men the showbread of the Tent (Tabernacle) to eat, for they were very hungry. When Saul heard about it, he killed the priest and all his family (1Sa 21-22). Then David fled to Achish king of Gath, a Philistine city. There he feigned madness so they wouldn't kill him, for David had the reputation of killing 10,000 to Saul's 1,000 (1Sa 21:10-15).

Then David left there and escaped to the cave of Adullam, and when his brothers and all his father's house heard of it, they went to him there. Also, everyone who was in distress, in debt or feeling bitter gathered to him, so he became their head, about 400 men (1Sa 22:1-2).

One time when David and his men were hiding in a cave, Saul went into the cave to relieve himself, but didn't see David and his men. David's men wanted David to kill Saul, but instead David cut of the corner of Saul's robe. Then he felt guilty for doing so and said to his men:

> *"Far be it from me, by Yahuah, that I should do this matter to my master, anointed of Yahuah, to stretch out my hand against him, for he is the anointed of Yahuah"* (1Sa 24:6).

David understood authority.

Afterwards David stood at a distance from Saul and told him that he could have killed him, but didn't. This proved that he wasn't Saul's enemy as Saul believed, so why was Saul chasing after him to kill him? Saul agreed that he was in the wrong, and then went home (1Sa 24:8-22).

David and Abigail (1Sa 25)

Abigail means "my father is joy." She was married to a wicked man named Nabal, which means "fool." He was rich with 3,000 sheep and 1,000 goats, and David and his men had been protecting the flock and Nabal's servants from harm. Because of this, David expected kindness when asking Nabal for some food. When Nabal refused and spoke harshly to David's servants, David took about 400 men to attack Nabal and kill every male belonging to him.

When Abigail heard about what her husband had done and what David was planning to do in retaliation, without telling Nabal, she rushed to David with food, apologized for her husband, and calmed David's anger. Ten days later Yahuah killed Nabal, and when David heard Nabal was dead, he thanked Abigail for stopping him from taking vengeance, and took her as wife.

David in Ziklag (1Sa 27)

To escape from Saul's relentless search to find and kill him, David went to the land of the Philistines and got permission from Achish, king of Gath, to have the city of Ziklag, some miles to the south, as his home and headquarters. He stayed there for a year and four months, and while there he raided the tribes south of him, leaving neither man nor woman alive to tell what he was doing. This was his practice all the days he lived in the country of the Philistines (1Sa 27:9, 11). When Achish would ask David what he was doing, David would say he was raiding south of Judah instead of what he was really doing. So Achish thought Israel hated David.

Saul and the medium at Endor (1Sa 28)

One time when king Saul saw the size of the Philistine army coming against him he was afraid and inquired of Yahuah to tell him what to do, but Yahuah wouldn't answer, either by dreams or by Urim* or by the prophets (1Sa 28:6). Samuel had died and Saul had put away the mediums and the spiritists from the land. But Saul found a woman medium at Endor and, disguising himself, he went to her and asked her to bring up Samuel. When Samuel came up, he told Saul that Yahuah would give the army of Israel into the hand of the Philistines and that Saul and his sons would join him in the grave *"tomorrow"* (1Sa 28:19).

> *The Urim and Thummim was a priestly device for obtaining oracles. On the high priest's ephod (an apron-like garment) lay a breastpiece – a pouch inlaid with 12 precious stones engraved with the names of the 12 tribes of Israel – that held the Urim and Thummim (Ex. 28:15–30; Lev. 8:8). By means of the Urim, the priest inquired of YHWH [Yahuah] on behalf of the ruler (Num. 27:21; cf. Yoma 7:5, "only for the king, the high court, or someone serving a need of the community"); they were one of the three legitimate means of obtaining oracles in early Israel (Urim, dreams, prophets; I Sam. 28:6). (jewishvirtuallibrary.org/the-urim-and-thummim)

The Philistines mistrust David (1Sa 29)

When the Philistine armies were gathering to do battle against Israel, Achish (king of Gath) and David were coming up at the rear. When the princes of the Philistines saw David, they demanded that he not come along because he might turn on them in the battle and fight for Israel. So David returned to Ziklag.

Ziklag and Amalek (1Sa 30)

When he and his men returned to Ziklag, they discovered that Amalek had destroyed Ziklag and taken captive everyone in it. When David and his men saw what happened, in their grief, they spoke of stoning David. But David with his men went after Amalek, killed them all, rescued all the wives and children that had been taken captive plus their belongings, and gained much spoil. And David shared the spoil among his army, and sent some of it as presents to the elders of Judah.

Saul commits suicide (1Sa 31)

In the meantime, the Philistines were defeating Israel and killed three of Saul's sons, including Jonathan, the close friend of David. Saul himself was mortally wounded by an arrow, and not wanting it said that uncircumcised men had killed him, he fell on his own sword and died. When the men of Israel who were beyond the valley and those who were beyond the Jordan heard that Saul and his sons were dead and that his men had fled, they forsook the cities and also fled, and the Philistines came and dwelt in them (1Sa 31:7).

In our survey of First Samuel we saw the birth of Samuel and followed him to his death, we saw the Box of Elohim captured and returned, we saw the reign of king Saul to his death, and we saw David anointed by Samuel and mature as a leader. We next turn to Second Samuel to follow the rest of David's life to his death.

5. Second Samuel. 8. First Chronicles

ORIGINALLY FIRST AND SECOND SAMUEL were one book. The book of First Chronicles recounts the same period of history as Second Samuel, but from a priestly perspective. So as we go through Second Samuel, occasionally something from First Chronicles will be noted.

We begin by seeing David's reaction of deep sorrow at the news of the defeat of Israel, and particularly the death of Saul and his sons. In the lament that he wrote regarding Saul and Jonathan, we have these words:

> *Declare it not in Gath,*
> *Proclaim it not in the streets of Ashkelon,*
> *Lest the daughters of the Philistines rejoice,*
> *Lest the daughters of the uncircumcised rejoice* (2Sa 1:20).

David anointed king at Hebron of Judah (2Sa 2-5)

Because Saul is dead, David went to Hebron where the men of Judah anointed him king over the house (tribe) of Judah. But the youngest of Saul's four sons was still alive, by name of Ishbosheth, and he was heir to his father's throne. So Abner, the commander of Saul's army, set him up to be king over all Israel. Only Judah followed David. As the warring between the house of Saul and the house of David continued, David's grew stronger while Saul's grew weaker (2Sa 3:1).

After awhile Ishbosheth insulted Abner, the commander of Israel's army, by accusing him of going into his father's concubine. Because of that, Abner decided to give Israel to David, and after meeting with David, he departed in peace. Joab, the commander of Judah's army, didn't like it, and murdered Abner for killing his brother. When David heard of the murder, he declared his innocence in the matter and put a curse on the house of Joab (2Sa 3:28-29).

After that, two of Ishbosheth's commanders killed Ishbosheth while he was in his bed and brought his head to David, expecting a reward. Instead, David had them executed for the wicked thing they had done. Then all the elders of Israel came to David at Hebron and anointed him sovereign over Israel. He was 30 years old when he began to rule, and he ruled 40 years—7½ years in Hebron over Judah, and 33 years over all Israel and Judah in Jerusalem (2Sa 5:4-5).

David makes Zion his city and brings the ark (2Sa 6-7)

David's first battle of the united kingdom was to capture the stronghold of Zion, called the City of David and Jerusalem. These three names all refer to the same city. After David had his house built there, he went to get the Box of Elohim (2Sa 6:2). Instead of following the Torah (Law), which required that the Box to be carried by the priests with poles on their shoulders, they put the Box on a new wagon and had it pulled by some oxen with priests leading the way. As they were bringing it, David and all the house of Israel were dancing before Yahuah.

On their way the oxen stumbled, and Uzzah reached out to keep the Box from falling. For this fault of touching the Box, Elohim killed him. This made David afraid of Yahuah, and he decided to leave it at the house of Obed-edom the Gittite, where it remained for three months. During that time Yahuah blessed Obed-edom and all his house. When David heard of the blessing, he was no longer afraid. and continued bringing the Box to the City of David, but this time they did it in the right way, the priests carrying it with the poles on their shoulders (1Ch 15:1-2, 15).

They were proceeding with much rejoicing, and when Michal, daughter of Saul and wife of David, saw her husband leaping and dancing before Yahuah, she despised him in her heart. As a result, she was barren to the day of her death.

David plans to build a Temple (2Sa 7)

After the kingdom was settled and at rest from their enemies, David wanted to build a house for Yahuah. In response, through the prophet Nathan, Yahuah told him that his desire was good, but it was for one of his seed to build it after he died. That would be Solomon, a son yet to be born.

David's sin with Bathsheba (2Sa 11-12)

We are skipping over the stories of many battles to the story of Bathsheba. She became pregnant through adultery with David while her husband Uriah (oo-ree-YAH) was away at war. To cover up the deed, he had Uriah murdered by putting him in a position on the battle front where he died. When her mourning for her husband was over, David took her as one of his wives and she bore him a son.

> *But the deed that David had done was evil in the eyes of Yahuah* (2Sa 11:27).

Then Yahuah sent the prophet Nathan to David telling him that because of this evil thing he did he would always be at war. Further, evil would come from his own house in which his neighbor (it would be Absalom, one of his sons) would lie with his wives in the sight of the sun. David repented (see Ps 51), but although he would not die, the child to be born from Bathsheba would die (2Sa 12:9-14).

A spiritual lesson: We reap the consequences of our sin even if the sin is forgiven.

After the child died, Bathsheba bore David a son whom she named Solomon. And Yahuah loved him (2Sa 12:24).

Absalom's rebellion and death (2Sa 13-18)

Ammon, a son of David, raped Tamar his half-sister and full sister of Absalom, another son of David. David was angry when he heard about it, but did not punish Ammon. Two years later, Ammon was killed by the command of Absalom, and Absalom fled to Geshur (a city east of the Sea of Galilee).

Later, after returning from Geshur *"Abshalom stole the hearts of the men of Israel"* (2Sa 15:6), and in Hebron had himself proclaimed king. When David found out, he fled from Jerusalem with his household and the men who were with him from Gath. But he left behind ten women, concubines, to look after the house.

When Absalom arrived in Jerusalem:

> *They pitched a tent for Absalom on the top of the house, and Absalom went in to his father's concubines before the eyes of all Israel* (2Sa 16:22).

Then Absalom with his army went after David, but by this time David and his servants were rested after their hasty flight from Jerusalem and were ready to fight (2Sa 18:1). David didn't want Absalom killed in the battle, but Joab, David's commander, disobeyed and killed him anyway (2Sa 18:6-9). And David wept bitterly over his son.

Judgment for numbering Israel (2Sa 24)

This chapter records that Yahuah moved on David to number the fighting men of Israel and Judah. Yahuah did this so that he might bring judgment on them for their idolatry (2Sa 24:1). However, because it was wrong for him to do the numbering, he repented, acknowledging that what he had done was foolish (2Sa 24:10).

In reply, Yahuah let David choose which of three punishments should happen: seven years of famine in the land, be pursued by his enemies for three months, or three days of plague in the land, all of it from Dan in the north to Beersheba in the south. David chose the third option. As a result, 70,000 men of the people died (2Sa 24:15).

The plague stopped when David bought the threshing floor of Araunah the Jebusite at Jerusalem.

> And David built an altar to Yahuah there and offered burnt offerings and peace offerings. And Yahuah answered the prayers for the land and the plague was withdrawn from Israel (2Sa 24:25).

Preparations for building the temple (1Ch)

The book of First Chronicles adds information about how David made extensive preparations for the building of the temple that Solomon would build. Yahuah had given David the architectural design for the temple, and David prepared all the necessary materials, and commanded all the rulers of Israel to help in the building so that as soon as Solomon succeeded him as king he could begin the construction. David also set up the worship system and temple service with the priests and the Levites.

Second Samuel ends when David is old, and First Kings begins with the circumstances of his death and how Solomon succeeded him as king. First Chronicles, on the other hand, ends with David's death and Solomon succeeding him as king.

Another item should be noted regarding Chronicles. Chronicles records only that which is positive about David. This is the heavenly perspective of our lives. When we repent of our sins and truly turn our hearts to the Father, all our sins are washed away as though they had never been.

This finishes our look at Second Samuel and First Chronicles. In our survey of the life of David in these books, we have seen his lament over the death of Saul, his being installed as king in Saul's stead, some of his battles, some of his sins, some of the judgment that came on him because of his sins, his quick repentance over his sins, and his contribution to the building and operation of the temple and to temple worship. Truly he was a man after Yahuah's own heart!

6. First Kings. 9. Second Chronicles

AS WE GO THROUGH FIRST KINGS, from time to time other information from Second Chronicles will be noted. The first eleven chapters of First Kings gives us the story of Solomon, of how he became king, of his rise to fame, and of his spiritual and moral decline that led to the dividing of the kingdom after his death. The rest of First Kings gives the stories of each of the kings of the divided kingdom up to the reign of Ahaziah in Israel.

As we go through First Kings we will see a common theme that by now is very familiar; namely, constant rebellion against Yahuah with only a few times of repentance. They rebelled by leaving the worship of Yahuah and following the idolatrous worship of the nations around them. In the northern kingdom, or Israel, there was not one righteous king. And because of repeated coups, there were several dynasties. (A dynasty is a succession of rulers from the same family.)

In the southern kingdom, or Judah, there were a few righteous kings, but the dynasty of David remained the same. By righteous is meant obeying the Torah (Law). It was through these kings that the Messianic line was carried, even though most of them were wicked.

Solomon succeeds David as king (1Ki 1-2)

We begin with David being old, unable to keep warm, and about to die. The solution his servants came up with to keep him warm was the body heat of a beautiful young maiden. They looked throughout the land and selected Abishag, a beautiful girl of Shunam, and brought her to the king to be his wife. She took care of him, but they had no intimate relations (1Ki 1:3-4); that is, although she became a queen, she remained a virgin.

In the meantime Adonijah, one of the sons of David from one of David's many wives, conspired with Joab (David's commander) and with Ebiathar (the high priest), and he proclaimed himself king in the place of his father David. He knew, of course, that his father had already promised that Solomon would be his heir, so this meant he would kill both Solomon and Bathsheba, Solomon's mother.

When David learned of this event, he immediately set in motion the coronation of Solomon as king over Israel (1Ki 1:39).

This ended Adonijah's attempt at the throne, and he deserved death for what he did, but Solomon said:

> *"If he shows himself to be a worthy man, not a hair of his head will fall to the earth; but if evil is found in him, he shall die"* (1Ki 1:52).

But evil was soon found in Adonijah. Through Bathsheba he asked Solomon that Abishag be given to him (Adonijah) as wife. Solomon recognized that this request was the same as asking to be king in the place of Solomon. So he had both Adonijah and Joab executed. And he dismissed Ebiathar from being high priest and gave the position to Zadok.

Yahuah grants Solomon wisdom and riches (1Ki 3)

After Solomon had secured himself as king, Yahuah appeared to him in a dream and said, *"Ask for what I shall give you"* (1Ki 3:5). In his reply, Solomon asked for an understanding heart to judge Yahuah's people and to discern between good and evil (1Ki 3:9).

Because Solomon hadn't asked for long life or riches, Yahuah said not only would he give him what he asked for so that he would be wiser than any before or after him, but also riches and esteem greater than all other kings during his days (1Ki 3:12-13). As for long life, however, it would only be if he walked according to Yahuah's ways as his father David had walked.

The first account of wisdom had to do with two prostitutes. They lived in the same house and both bore sons, three days apart. But one in her sleep rolled over on her baby and it died, and so she switched babies while the other mother was still asleep. The other, when she examined the dead baby, realized it wasn't hers. So they both came before Solomon, each claiming the live baby.

To solve who was the real mother, Solomon had a sword brought to him and ordered that the living child be cut in two, each woman getting half. The real mother, because of compassion for her son, asked that the child not be killed but be given to the other. The other declined, wanting the child cut in two. This showed who the real mother was, and Solomon commanded that the child be given to the first woman. As a result:

> *All Israel heard of the judgment which the king had rendered. And they feared the king, for they saw that the wisdom of Elohim was in him to do judgment* (1Ki 3:28).

Solomon has the temple built (1Ki 6-8; 2Ch 7:1-3)

After this, Solomon built the temple and had all the furniture and the Box of the Covenant brought into it. The temple was the same proportion as the Tent (Tabernacle), except it was twice the size. Regarding the Box, only the two tablets of stone were in it. No information is given regarding what happened to the pot of manna and Aaron's rod that budded.

When the temple was dedicated, the esteem of Yahuah as a cloud filled the place so that the priests were unable to stand and perform the service (1Ki 8:10-11; 2Ch 7:1-3).

The queen of Sheba is amazed (1Ki 10)

In this account we can see Solomon as a type of Messiah and the queen of Sheba a type of the bride. She had heard the report of Solomon and came to test him with hard questions (1Ki 10:1). But when she saw his wealth and wisdom, she said she hadn't believed it to be true until she saw it, and what she saw was far greater than the report she had heard (1Ki 10:6-7). And Solomon gave her all she desired (1Ki 10:13).

The moral and spiritual decline of Solomon (1Ki 11)

Solomon married many women of the pagan nations and built altars for them, and they turned away his heart from Yahuah. As a result, Yahuah told him he would remove the kingdom from him and give it to his servant, but not during his lifetime, for the sake of his father David. Only the tribe of Judah would remain with him for the sake of his servant David and for the sake of Jerusalem which he has chosen (1Ki 11:11-13).

By this time the tribe of Benjamin was within the boundaries of Judah, so this made two tribes that would make up the southern kingdom after Solomon's death. The Levites, the priestly tribe, were located in cities throughout Israel, but after the split they were forced out of the northern kingdom and lived in Judah.

So Yahuah raised up adversaries against Solomon. Among them was Jeroboam. The prophet Ahijah prophesied over him that he would became king of the ten northern tribes after Solomon's death. When Solomon heard of it, he sought to kill Jeroboam, but Jeroboam fled to Egypt and stayed there until Solomon died. Thus ends Solomon's reign. It lasted 40 years, the same as his father David's and the same as Saul's.

Jeroboam, king of the northern kingdom, Israel (1Ki 12-13)

The kingdom split in this way. All Israel came to Shekem to set up Rehoboam, the son of Solomon, as king. Jeroboam also came, now that Solomon was dead. The elders of Israel told Rehoboam that if he would lighten their load of taxes and compulsory labor they would serve him. When Rehoboam replied that he would increase their load, the ten northern tribes revolted and set up their own nation with Jeroboam as their king. Only Judah and Benjamin remained with Rehoboam the son of Solomon.

> Because of confusion regarding the names Jeroboam and Rehoboam, as a reminder, sometimes the names of kingdoms are noted with the names of the kings.

Yahuah had told Jeroboam (northern kingdom, Israel) that if he would obey Yahuah that his kingdom would be established, but if he disobeyed it would be taken away from him. But Jeroboam didn't heed the warning. Jerusalem was the center of worship where

Yahuah had commanded that all adult males of Israel were to assemble for the annual feasts. Because of this, Jeroboam was afraid that his people would kill him and go back to Rehoboam of the house of David. So he made his own religion by making two calves of gold and telling his people that these elohim were those which brought them out of Egypt. And he made priests from all sorts of people who were not of the tribe of Levi (1Ki 12:28-31).

One day when king Jeroboam (northern kingdom) was standing by the altar in Bethel to make an offering, a man of Elohim from Judah (southern kingdom) prophesied against the altar saying:

> *"Altar, altar! This is what Yahuah says: 'Behold, a son named Josiah will be born to the house of David. On you he will slay the priests of the high places who now burn incense here, and human bones will be burned on you'"* (1Ki 13:2).

(This prophesy was fulfilled 340 years later.)

This prophet also gave a sign to prove that the prophecy was from Elohim, that the altar would split apart and the ashes poured out. When king Jeroboam heard the words, he stretched out his hand and commanded that the prophet be seized. But while his hand was stretched out it dried up so he couldn't bring it back, and the altar split apart and the ashes poured out. The king then asked the man of Elohim to pray for him that his hand be restored, and it was (1Ki 13:1-6).

The king then invited the man of Elohim to his home for some refreshment and a gift. But the man of Elohim refused, saying Yahuah had forbidden him to do so and to return immediately. When an old prophet in Bethel heard what happened, he hastened after the man of Elohim and invited him to come back to Bethel with him. Again the man of Elohim refused. But the old prophet lied to him, saying he was also a prophet and a messenger (angel) told him to bring the man of Elohim back with him to his house for some bread and water (1Ki 13:18).

The man of Elohim believed the old prophet and obeyed the lie. As judgment for disobedience to Elohim, while he was again on the road back to Judah, this time on a donkey, a lion killed him. When the old prophet heard about it, he went and found the body with the donkey and the lion standing by. The lion hadn't eaten the body or harmed the donkey (1Ki 13:28).

So this was another sign to king Jeroboam that what the man of Elohim prophesied was truly from Yahuah and what he said would surely happen. Even though Jeroboam saw all this and knew it was from Yahuah, he didn't repent, and continued with his false religion, ordaining whomever he wished to be priests of the high places.

> *And this matter was the sin of the house of Jeroboam, even to cut it off and destroy it from the face of the earth* (1Ki 13:34).

Frequently we find in the book of Kings the reference to this sin, for all the kings of Israel (also called Samaria and the northern kingdom) followed this sin, and all were cut off for the same reason.

One result of the sin of Jeroboam was that all the priests and Levites who were in Israel left their homes and came to Judah and Jerusalem, because Jeroboam and his sons rejected them from serving as priests to Yahuah. Then, after they left, all others of Israel as set their heart to seek Yahuah also came to Judah and Jerusalem. This is a type of the bride of Messiah leaving lukewarm and apostate churches to join assemblies that are truly following Yahushua.

The idolatry of Judah and judgment through Egypt (1Ki 14:21-28)

So how was Judah doing during this time? Not good! They also provoked Yahuah to jealousy with their sins, even more than their fathers had done. For they built high places and pillars and Asherim on every high hill and under every green tree, and also had cult prostitutes according to all the evil of the nations which Yahuah had dispossessed before Israel when they came into the land (1Ki 14:22-24).

> Asherah, pl. Asherim, the stem of a tree deprived of its boughs, and rudely shaped into an image, and planted in the ground. (Easton's Bible Dictionary)

So Yahuah sent Sheshak king of Egypt against Jerusalem, and he took away the treasures of the temple and the king's house and also the shields of gold which Solomon had made (1Ki 14:26).

Ahab of Israel and Elijah the prophet (1Ki 16:29 – 22:40)

We skip over a few kings in both the southern and northern kingdoms and come to king Ahab of Israel. He was evil like the kings before him but went even further than they, in that he married

Jezebel, daughter of Ethbaal king of the Sidonians, and began to serve Baal and revere him (1Ki 16:31).

This brings us to the prophet Elijah. His name means "Yahuah is my Elohim" or "Yahuah is Elohim." He told Ahab that there would be no dew or rain except at his word (1Ki 17:1). Then Elijah hid by the wadi Kerith, and Yahuah sent ravens to feed him. (A wadi is a valley with a stream that dries up when there is no rain.) When the stream dried up Yahuah sent Elijah to a widow in Zarephath of Sidon whom Yahuah had commanded to sustain him. When Elijah arrived, the widow was preparing her last meal for herself and her son before dying from starvation. But Elijah asked that she give him bread and water first, saying by the word of Yahuah:

> *"The container of flour shall not finish, nor the jar of oil be lessened, until the day Yahuah sends rain on the earth"* (1Ki 17:14).

Later the widow's son died, and she turned to Elijah for help. He prayed to Yahuah, and the child lived. Then she knew that he was a man of Elohim and that the word of Yahuah in his mouth is truth (1Ki 17:24).

When the drought was in its third year, at Elijah's command Ahab gathered all Israel on Mount Carmel, plus the 450 prophets of Baal and the 400 prophets of Asherah who eat at Jezebel's table. He asked the people how long would they dance between two opinions. *"If Yahuah is Elohim, follow him; and if Baal, follow him."* But the people didn't answer (1Ki 18:21).

The test would be an answer by fire from the true Elohim. The prophets of Baal went first. They set up their altar with wood and a slain bull and called on the name of Baal their elohim to provide the fire. But no fire came. After some time of failure, Elijah said it was his turn. He built an altar in the name of Yahuah, made a large trench around it, placed the wood and a slain bull on it, and had lots of water poured over it all. Then he prayed, asking Yahuah to let the people know that he is Yahuah Elohim, and that he turn their hearts back to him again.

> *Then the fire of Yahuah fell and consumed the burnt offering, the wood and the stones and the dust, and licked up the water that was in the trench. When all the people saw, they fell on their*

faces, and said, "Yahuah, he is the Elohim! Yahuah, he is the Elohim!" (1Ki 18:38-39).

Then Elijah killed all the false prophets, prayed for rain, and rain came. Then, because Jezebel swore to kill him for killing her prophets, he fled to Horeb where the Torah (Law) had been given, entered a cave, and in despondency asked Yahuah to kill him. Instead, Yahuah told him to anoint Hazael as sovereign over Aram (Syria), to anoint Jehu as king over Israel, and to anoint Elisha as prophet to replace him (1Ki 18:40 - 19:16).

The next event we look at is the story of Naboth's vineyard. Ahab wanted it because it was next to his house. When Naboth wouldn't sell it, Ahab became depressed and wouldn't eat. Jezebel then got the vineyard for Ahab by having Naboth falsely accused of blasphemy and stoned to death. Elijah then prophesied of the death of Ahab and Jezebel. In response, Ahab humbled himself before Yahuah by putting on sackcloth, fasting, lying in sackcloth, and going about softly. As a result of this humbling, Yahuah wouldn't bring the evil in his days, but in the days of his son (1Ki 21:27-29).

But evil was brought on Ahab himself. In a battle with Aram at Ramoth Gilead, Ahab was mortally wounded by an arrow that pierced between the joints of his armor and blood ran out from the wound onto the floor of the chariot. And when the chariot was washed, dogs licked up his blood, according to the word of Yahuah (1Ki 22:38).

Jehoshaphat of Judah (2Ch 17:3; 20:15-25)

Second Chronicles says this of Jehoshaphat. He was one of the righteous kings, for he walked in the former ways of his father David and did not seek the Baals, so Yahuah was with him (2Ch 17:3).

There came a time when Ammon, Moab and Mount Seir joined together to fight against Jehoshaphat. He became afraid and prayed to Yahuah for help. Yahuah told him not to be afraid of that great army, because the battle isn't his, but Elohim's. They were just to position themselves, stand still, and see the deliverance of Yahuah. So Jeho-shaphat appointed singers to go ahead of the army and praise Yahuah. Then Yahuah caused the enemy to fight and destroy one another, so that all were dead (2Ch 20:15-25).

Ahaziah of Israel (1Ki 22:51-53)

First Kings ends with the reign of Ahaziah over Israel, son of Ahab. His story ends with these words, words which apply to all the kings of Israel.

> *He did evil in the eyes of Yahuah and walked in the way of his father (Ahab) and in the way of his mother (Jezebel) and in the way of Jeroboam son of Nebat who had made Israel sin, and served Baal and bowed himself to it and provoked Yahuah Elohim of Israel according to all that his father (Ahab) had done* (1Ki 22:52-53).

This ends our survey of First Kings with some parallel accounts in Second Chronicles. We have seen the rise and fall of Solomon, the dividing of the kingdom into north and south, and some key people in those kingdoms. We next go to Second Kings with some parallel accounts in Second Chronicles.

7. Second Kings. 9. Second Chronicles

As WE BEGIN THE BOOK OF SECOND KINGS, keep in mind that in the Hebrew Old Covenant scriptures First and Second Kings are one book, just as First and Second Samuel and First and Second Chronicles are each one book. It was when they were translated into Greek in the Greek Septuagint that they were divided, and that division came into our scriptures as well. So the story line moves directly from one to the other without a break.

How Ahaziah king of Israel dies (2Ki 1:1-16)

In the closing words of First Kings we saw the summary of the life of king Ahaziah who succeeded his father Ahab in Israel. In the opening words of Second Kings we have the story of how Ahaziah died. When he injured himself in a fall in his house in Samaria, he sent messengers to inquire of Baal-Zebub (a name that means the fly-god, or master of flies, or Lord of the Flies), the god of Ekron, to ask if he would recover from the injury .

While the messengers were on their way, Yahuah told Elijah to meet the messengers from Ahaziah and say that indeed Ahaziah would die. The messengers therefore returned to Ahaziah more quickly than expected and described Elijah this way:

> *"He was a hairy man, and wore a leather girdle around his waist"* (2Ki 1:8).

From the description Ahaziah knew it was Elijah. So he sent a captain with 50 soldiers to get Elijah. But when they came, a fire from Elohim came down and consumed them all. So Ahaziah sent another captain with 50 soldiers to get Elijah, and they also died the same way. However, when Ahaziah a third time sent a captain with 50 soldiers to get Elijah, this third captain begged for mercy. So Elijah went with them and said to Ahaziah:

> *"Thus said Yahuah, 'Because you have sent messengers to inquire of Baal-Zebub, the elohim of Ekron, is it because there is no Elohim in Israel to inquire of his word? Therefore you are not going to get out of the bed to which you have gone up, for you shall certainly die'"* (2Ki 1:16).

Elisha (2Ki 2–8)

Chapter two of Second Kings gives the story of Elijah transferring his anointing to Elisha and then ascending to heaven in a whirlwind. Before leaving, Elijah asked Elisha what he wanted, and Elisha asked for a double portion of Elijah's spirit (2Ki 2:1-12). In type, Elijah represents Messiah who has gone to heaven but he has delegated authority to his assembly, the bride, and said that his believers would do greater things than he did. So Elisha is a type of the bride. He does similar miracles to Elijah, but also more.

Elisha gets Elijah's mantel and strikes the Jordan River with it, and the river divides so he can cross over on dry ground (2Ki: 2:13-14). In Jericho, Elisha throws salt into a polluted water source and it becomes pure (2Ki 2:19-22). And when some young men mock him, they are killed by two she-bears (2Ki 2:23-24).

Elisha is now the head of the school of prophets, succeeding Elijah in that position. Chapters 4 to 7 record many miracles Elisha did.

- A widow was able to pay her debt by a miraculous supply of oil (2Ki 4:1-7).
- A dead boy was brought back to life (2Ki 4:18-37).
- Flour put in a pot of poisonous stew made it safe (2Ki 4:38-41).

- Food for twenty people fed 100 with some left over (2Ki 4:42-44).
- Naaman the Aramean was healed from leprosy (2Ki 5:1-14).
- A stick thrown in water caused an axe head to float (2Ki 6:1-7).
- The Aramean army that was besieging Samaria became so terrified that they all fled leaving all their belongings behind (2Ki 7).

Jehu of Israel and Athaliah of Judah (2Ki 9 - 10)

In chapters 9-10 Jehu is anointed king over Israel and told to completely destroy the house of Ahab, which included all his 70 sons and his wife Jezebel. And so he did. Then he killed all the prophets of Baal and destroyed all images of Baal. But he still bowed to the golden calves that Jeroboam, the first king of Israel, had set up.

This coup in Israel also affected Judah, because the king of Judah, Jehoram, had married Athaliah, the daughter of Ahab and Jezebel. Jehoram died of a horrible disease, and Ahaziah his son (and Athaliah's son) was killed by Jehu during the coup in Israel. Athaliah was like her mother Jezebel and was the one who really ruled. So when she saw that her son Ahaziah was dead, she took the throne and killed all the sons of her late husband; that is, all the possible heirs to the throne.

> Names are confusing because many of the kings in both the north and the south had the same names, and sometimes they were ruling at the same time.

Joash of Judah (2Ki 11 – 12)

But the youngest son, Joash, a one-year old baby, was hidden. Six years later, the priest Jehoiada with the help of a sizeable guard, proclaimed Joash as king and had Athaliah killed and had all the Baal worship that Athaliah had set up destroyed (2Ki 11). Joash also had the temple repaired (2Ki 12:4-16).

As long as Jehoiada lived, he guided Joash in ruling the right way. But when Jehoiada died, Joash and all the people of Judah went back into idolatry. When Zekariah, the son of Jehoiada, told them that Yahuah would judge them for their sin, the people stoned Zekariah to death (2Ch 24:20).

The end of Israel (2Ki 17)

After this there came many wars against Israel and against Judah because of their wickedness. We jump over all of these and the various kings and nations involved in them and come to the end of Israel, the northern kingdom. The king of Assyria captured Samaria and exiled them to Assyria and in the cities of the Medes (2Ki 17:5-6).

It was the policy of the king of Assyria when conquering a nation to deport all survivors into other lands and replace them with survivors from those other lands. That's what the king of Assyria did with Samaria. But the immigrants to the land of the northern kingdom encountered a problem. Yahuah sent lions among them which kept on killing among them. The immigrants concluded that the reason for the lions was that they didn't know what the elohim of the land required of them. So one of the priests who had been exiled from Samaria was sent back to teach them how to fear Yahuah (2Ki 17:28).

Keep in mind, though, that this priest wasn't a Levite, and the kind of worship that he knew was the false worship of the golden calves. So the immigrants added this false worship to their own pagan worship.

> *They revered Yahuah, and served their own elohim according to the ruling of the nations from among whom they had been exiled* (2Ki 17:33).

Hezekiah (2Ki 18 - 19)

The rest of Second Kings deals with the surviving kingdom of Judah. We will look only at a few kings, and we start with Hezekiah, a righteous king. His reign began a few years before the end of the northern kingdom.

> *He took away the high places, and broke the pillars and cut down the Asherah, and broke in pieces the bronze serpent which Moses had made, for until those days the children of Israel burned incense to it* (2Ki 18:4).

He also had the temple repaired and the priestly responsibilities restored, and then called all Israel and Judah to celebrate the Passover (2Ch 29 - 31). We saw earlier that when Jeroboam became king of Israel he set up his own worship system with his own priests and that the Levites left Israel and came to Judah. At this call to the Passover by Hezekiah, all those in Israel who wanted true worship came to Judah. It was shortly after that that Assyria took Israel captive. Hezekiah's call to come to the Passover is a type of the last-day call of the bride to the assembly to come out of Babylon; that is, out of lukewarmness and false doctrines and practices before the rapture of the bride believers, and the tribulation of the lukewarm believers that follows.

Assyria, after taking Israel, also captured all the walled cities of Judah and then came against Jerusalem. The prophet Isaiah was in Jerusalem at this time, and he told Hezekiah not to worry, but that Yahuah himself would defend the city and the Assyrian army would go home. That night a messenger of Yahuah killed 185,000 of their army, and the rest of the army left. And soon after that two of the sons of the Assyrian king killed their father (2Ki 18 - 19).

Josiah of Judah (2Ki 22-23)

Three kings later we come to Josiah. The two kings before him (his father and grandfather) had reversed all the reforms that Hezekiah had done. In fact, the people rejoiced to go back to idolatry. But Josiah had a different heart. While the temple was being repaired, the Book of the Torah (Law) was found. Josiah believed the cursings for idolatry recorded in it, and so he renewed the covenant with the people and had all the idolatry removed (2Ki 23:15-16). (See 1Ki 13:1-3 where the prophecy was made.) As his great-grandfather Hezekiah before him had done during his reform, Josiah held the Passover. It was the greatest Passover ever held (2Ch 35:17-18).

Josiah was the last righteous king in Judah. All the following kings were wicked, and the people themselves were just as wicked. As with Hezekiah, the reform of Josiah never changed the people. It was a reform forced on the people, and as soon as Josiah died, they went back to their idolatry (2Ki 23).

The end of Judah (2Ki 24)

Yahuah sent king Nebuchadnezzar of Babylon to end the kingdom of Judah. There were three deportations of people, and then the city and the temple were destroyed. Then Nebuchadnezzar appointed Gedaliah as governor over the remaining people in the land. But when Gedaliah was assassinated, they all fled to Egypt, taking the prophet

Jeremiah with them.

In the book of Jeremiah we will see the prophet's life and his effect on the people during those years. One of his prophecies was that the captivity in Babylon would last 70 years, and after that they would return to Jerusalem. Because of this prophecy, Second Chronicles concludes with information that in the first year of Cyrus king of Persia Yahuah stirred up the spirit of Cyrus to have the temple in Jerusalem rebuilt, and he gave permission for any of the exiles who wanted to leave to do so (2Ch 36:22).

This ends our survey of Second Kings, and also of Second Chronicles. The rule of King David was the height of the kingdom, and from there on it was all downhill until its total destruction. Solomon backslid, the kingdom split, idolatry was the norm in the northern kingdom, which resulted in its destruction by Assyria, and idolatry soon became the norm in the southern kingdom, which resulted in its destruction by Babylon.

Moses warned the people of this before they entered the Promised Land, and the prophets continually warned the people of this throughout the years they were there, but the people would not listen. However, Moses and the prophets also said there would be a remnant that would truly be the people of Elohim. That is yet in the future. All of this is also a type of the assembly today.

We saw in the conclusion of Second Chronicles that a remnant returned from Babylon. In the next books we examine that.

10-12. Ezra, Nehemiah, Esther

THE BOOKS OF EZRA AND NEHEMIAH continue from Second Chronicles and have to do with the settling of the remnant back in Judah. In these two books we see the rebuilding of the temple and the Jerusalem city wall. We also see that the remnant that returned are in a bad spiritual condition, so these books are about spiritual reform as well. In fact, their spiritual condition affects the rebuilding of the temple and the city wall.

The book of Esther is an historical aside, because it is a personal story that takes place in Persia and occurs in the time period of Ezra and Nehemiah. In this respect it is similar to the book of Ruth which, as we saw earlier, is also an historical aside with a personal story that happened early on in the period of the Judges.

Ezra

The book of Ezra (ehz-RAW, means helper) begins by repeating the closing words of Second Chronicles. Note, it was Yahuah who stirred up Cyrus to proclaim that the Jews could return and rebuild the temple. But only about 50,000 of the estimated two million Jews responded to the proclamation. Who were these people that responded? They were *"all those whose spirits Elohim had stirred"* (Ezr 1:5). So we see that Yahuah moved on the political leader, and then moved on his chosen ones. Further, Cyrus sent back all the temple utensils that Nebuchadnezzar of Babylon had taken, and the Jewish exiles that stayed behind gave large donations to help in the building. This is a type of lukewarm believers helping the "hot" believers, the bride of Messiah.

The leaders of this first group that returned were Joshua (Heb Yahushua) the priest, and Zerubbabel (a prince in the Messianic line). The first thing that they rebuilt was the altar of burnt offering, then they performed the Festival of Booths. But it was not until two years later that they began rebuilding the temple, beginning with laying the foundation.

At this point we must remember what happened in the northern kingdom. Israel had been exiled by Assyria, foreigners had been brought in to replace them, and a priest (who was accustomed to worshiping golden calves) had been returned to show the foreigners how to worship the "god of the land." The descendents of these people were called *"the people of the land"* and later became known as Samaritans. When they saw the temple being rebuilt in Jerusalem, they came to Zerubbabel and Joshua the priest and offered to help in the building.

But Zerubbabel and Joshua and the rest of the heads of the fathers' houses of Israel told them no, but they alone will build to Yahuah the Elohim of Israel, as Cyrus the king of Persia had commanded. Also, the people of the land were weakening the hands of the people of Judah and troubling them in their building and hiring counselors against them to hinder their plans. They were doing this all the days of Cyrus, even until the reign of Darius king of Persia (Ezra 4:3-5).

In type, the *"people of the land"* are lukewarm believers who try to stop revival in any way they can, including having laws passed. And that is what happened here. Darius commanded that they stop the rebuilding, so they stopped. Then the prophets Haggai and Zechariah prophesied for them to continue building. So they restarted, despite the order of Darius. When Darius asked why they were disobeying, they said they were following the decree of Cyrus. After reading that decree, Darius ordered the temple rebuilding to continue and that all expenses be paid by the government and taxes of the people. And soon the temple was completed.

This completes part one of the book of Ezra, chapters 1-6.

Part two begins about 80 years later. Artaxerxes king of Persia sent Ezra the priest to Jerusalem with another group from Babylon with all expenses paid, and also with all authority to get whatever he needed from the local governor. Included in the decree were instructions to appoint magistrates and judges to judge the people, all such as knew the laws of their Elohim. And whoever fails to obey the laws of Elohim should be sentenced, whether to death, banishment, confiscation of goods, or imprisonment (Ezra 7:25-26).

After his arrival in Jerusalem, Ezra organized the priests and offerings and taught the people the Torah (Law) of Elohim. When Ezra found out that intermarriage had been going on, he ordered an examination as to who were involved, and then had those men put away their foreign wives.

> Ezra 10:17, 18-44. Barnes' Notes
> Verse 44. The guilty persons, it would seem, were 113 in number. They comprised 4 members of the high priest's family, 13 other priests, 10 Levites, and 86 lay Israelites belonging to at least 10 distinct families. (Barnes' Notes.)

Nehemiah

Nehemiah (means "consolation of Yahuah), a cupbearer for king Artaxerxes, was in Babylon when he heard news that things were not going well in Judah and that the wall of Jerusalem was broken down and the gates burned. After Nehemiah prayed and fasted regarding the problem, the king sent Nehemiah to Jerusalem to rebuild the wall.

After arriving, he organized the people so that each household had its own section of wall to repair.

In type, the wall is the protection of Yahuah for those who love him. So building the wall is a type of growing in our love for Yahuah and overcoming sin in our lives.

The nations of the land hated that the wall was being rebuilt, and conspired to fight. The chief persons of this conspiracy were Sanballat and Tobiah. They are a type of the world who want to destroy the work of Elohim. The promotion in the United States of atheism with its indoctrination of separation of church and state and of evolution is an example of this. To protect themselves from attack, the workers also carried weapons. Each one had his sword girded at his side as he built (Neh 4:18). Our weapon is the word of Elohim.

Besides the outward problem, there was also an inward problem. In type, the outward problem is the world, and the inward problem is worldliness in the church. The rich nobles among them were taking advantage of the poor. They were charging high interest on loans, and then foreclosing on their land so they had no food, and then making them slaves. Nehemiah told the nobles to give back their lands and their houses, including some of the silver and harvest they had taken from them (Neh 5:11). And they agreed. Also at that time the king appointed Nehemiah as governor over Judah.

Very few of the exiles who had returned lived in Jerusalem, most living outside in other cities of Judah. Besides, the buildings in Jerusalem had not been repaired. So when the wall was completed, it was arranged that one out of ten people would live in Jerusalem (Neh 11:1).

Nehemiah led several reforms to bring the people in line with the Torah. One was for them to separate the mixed multitude from Israel. Another was to do no work on the sabbath (Neh 13).

This ends our survey of Nehemiah. The "sons of the exile" had not had a change of heart as the result of being sent to Babylon because of their sin. By the time of Yahushua Messiah, they still hadn't had a change of heart. Nor have they had a change of heart to this day. But after the gentile church age is over a remnant of Israel will repent and have a true conversion. Some of the books of prophecy tell of this.

Esther

Esther is a Persian name meaning star. She was a Jewess named Hadassah, meaning myrtle (an evergreen shrub with fragrant white flowers), but was given the name Esther when she entered the royal harem. The events in this book took place in Persia among the descendants of the Jews who had been made captive by Babylonia and had not returned to Judah when given the opportunity.

The king made a feast which included a lot of drinking. The women had their own separate feast hosted by queen Vashti. When the king wanted to show off his lovely wife at the men's feast, she refused, which set a bad example for the women of the empire, for each man should be master of his own house. To replace the queen, a beauty contest was held throughout the empire, and those chosen as the most beautiful would be prepared to be presented to the king. Among the maidens chosen was Hadassah, the niece of Mordecai who was raising her, and whom she always obeyed. When she was chosen, Mordecai told her not to make her nationality known and to use her new name of Esther.

Eunuchs were in charge of the harem to which the maidens were brought for twelve months of preparation. Esther found favor with the head eunuch, and received the best preparation, and was chosen by the king to be his queen.

In the meantime the king elevated Haman, a prince, to be higher than all the princes in the empire, and commanded all his servants to bow to him. One of the servants was Mordecai who sat within the king's gate, and he refused to bow. When Haman found out that Mordecai was a Jew, he plotted not only to have Mordecai executed, but to have all the Jews in the empire killed. Haman went to the king with much money, and the king gave him authority to have all the Jews killed, young and old, little children and women, and to plunder their possessions. This was to be done all in one day, the thirteenth day of the twelfth month, the month of Adar (Est 3:13).

When Mordecai learned of the decree, he commanded Esther to go to the king and plead before him for her people. She agreed to go, even if it meant her death, for the law was that she could only come if sent for, upon pain of death, unless the king extended his scepter to her, which he did. When he asked her what she wanted, she asked to have a feast with just him, Haman and herself, and at that feast she asked for another feast in which she would reveal what she wanted. Haman was elated at being a guest, until Ester revealed what she wanted, that her life be given to her and that of her people. She explained to the king that she and her people had been sold to be destroyed (Est 7:3-4).

When the king asked who was doing this, she said, *"The adversary and enemy is this evil Haman!"* (Est 7:6).

Haman ended up being impaled on the same tall pole he had prepared for Mordecai; Mordecai was elevated to be second to the king; and the Jews were given permission to defend themselves on the day set for their own annihilation, and also to kill all their enemies. (By Persian law, once the king made a decree it could not be revoked.) It took two days to kill all their enemies, and those two days were declared to be an annual feast called Purim. Purim means casting lots, for Haman had cast lots to see on which day he would have all the Jews killed.

The story is full of types and has immense spiritual significance. Haman is a type of the devil, our adversary. Mordecai is a type of Elohim who gives wisdom to his people. The king is a type of Messiah who has all authority. Esther is a type of the bride of Messiah who has prepared herself to be his wife. And the chief eunuch is a type of the spirit of Elohim which instructs the bride how to become mature and ready for marriage.

FIVE POETRY BOOKS

HEBREW POETRY is different from English poetry. Except in the case of "free verse," English poetry is based on rhyme and rhythm. In contrast, Hebrew poetry is based on thoughts arranged in certain ways. One way is parallelism. It can be a parallel of an idea, in which both lines mean the same thing; or a parallel of expansion, in which the second line expands on the thought of the previous one; or a parallel of contrast, in which the second line gives an opposite idea. Examples of these will be given as we go along.

1. Job

THE BOOK OF JOB (rhymes with robe) begins and ends with prose, the rest being poetry. It is the story of a righteous man *"who feared Elohim and turned aside from evil"* (Job 1:1). He lived before the giving of the Torah (Law), perhaps during the time of Abraham.

Satan spoke against that righteousness, telling Elohim that Job was righteous only because Elohim protected him from harm, but that if that protection were removed, Job would curse Elohim. So Elohim gave Satan permission to destroy Job's property and to kill his children, and later to destroy his health (covered with boils), but he was not allowed to kill Job. When Job's three friends came to sympathize with him, then begins a conversation which is given in poetry.

Job's three friends were Eliphaz, Bildad and Zophar. These three believed whenever bad things happen to a person, it is because that person sinned; and also the opposite, if a person were righteous, no harm would come to him. Therefore, since Job was experiencing bad things, Elohim had brought this upon him because he had sinned. So they were telling Job to confess his sin and repent, and Elohim would restore him. In poetry form, each of the three tells Job this, and after each of their speeches, Job defends himself saying he is righteous and has nothing to repent of.

Job is confused. What the three were telling him he also once believed. But that belief is now shaken, for he knows he has always done what is right, and yet this calamity did happen. As the conversation continues, Job gets more and more frustrated. He wishes he had never been born. He wishes he had someone to plead his case to Elohim, then Elohim would stop this calamity.

Finally, the three men stopped answering Job because he was righteous in his own eyes. But there was another man there, much younger than they, by name of Elihu. He became angry with Job for justifying himself rather than Elohim.

> *He was also angry with the three friends, because they had found no way to refute Job, and yet had condemned him* (Job 32:3).

He told Job that he opens his mouth in vain, that he increases words without knowledge (notice the parallelism) (Job 35:2-4, 16).

104

After Elihu defends Elohim at great length, Yahuah himself speaks to Job. Yahuah goes at great length to show how great he is and how small and weak Job and mankind are (Job 38:2-5).

Job responds.

"Behold, I am insignificant, what would I answer you?
    I lay my hand upon my mouth.
  Once I have spoken, but I will not answer –
    And twice, but I will not continue" (Job 40:4-5).

"I have heard of you by the hearing of the ear,
    But now my eye sees you.
  Therefore I despise (myself),
    And repent in dust and ashes" (Job 42:5-6).

After this Yahuah ends Job's suffering and blesses him with much more than he had before—more children, more property, and more honor from his community.

Yahuah does not tell Job why his suffering came; it is enough to know that Elohim always does what is right. Through his ordeal, though, Job changed. He was righteous before because he was living according to all the light he had. But now he has more light. So no more would he ever declare himself to be more righteous than Elohim.

2. Psalms

THE BOOK OF PSALMS (actually five books combined into one book) expresses the whole range of human experience, and all of them center on how wonderful Elohim and his word are. It is a collection of songs written by many people over a period of about 1,000 years (Moses to Ezra). Of the 150 psalms, 73 are attributed to King David, 31 to others, and 46 anonymous.

The predominant themes are prayer and praise, but the Psalms cover a great variety of personal experiences. They are quoted more frequently in the New Testament than any other book except Isaiah. They are often called the Psalms of David because more come from him than from anyone else.

In our survey of Psalms we will look at a few of them that are representative of others. The first psalm is like an introduction to all the psalms. The Hebrew word for "instruction" is *torah*, and is usually translated as "law." But the word means more than law, it is instruction on how to live and has far more in it than laws.

Notice the parallelism in verse one, quoted below. Each succeeding line gives more information of what the blissful man is not, and in the process shows the downward path of the wicked. First, the blissful one doesn't pay attention to what the unrighteous want him to do. Second, he doesn't go further to agree with the lifestyle of sinners. And finally, he doesn't join them in attacking the righteous. The righteous person does what Elohim calls right. The unrighteous person does what man thinks is right.

> Most translations use "blessed" or "happy" instead of "blissful." The Hebrew is *esher* [eh-SHER], "a masculine noun meaning a person's state of bliss," (Strong's # 835, Word Study Dictionary OT.)

Blissful is the man who doesn't walk
> *in the counsel of the unrighteous*
> *Nor stand in the path of sinners*
> *Nor not sit in the seat of scoffers* (Ps 1:1).

The parallelism of the next verse adds information of what one does that shows his delight—he meditates.

But his delight is in the instruction of Yahuah,
> *And he meditates in his instruction day and night* (Ps 1:2).

The parallelism of the next verse shows why this man is blissful. He experiences prosperity in bearing fruit for the kingdom of Elohim; that is, the fruit of souls coming into the kingdom and in nurturing them to become the bride of Messiah.

For he shall be as a tree
> *Planted by the rivers of water*
> *That yields its fruit in its season*
> *And whose leaf does not wither*
> *And whatever he does prospers* (Ps 1:3).

The parallelism of the next two verses shows the destruction of those who choose unrighteousness.

The unrighteous are not so,
> *But are like the chaff which the wind blows away.*

> *Therefore the unrighteous shall not rise in the judgment,*
> *Nor sinners in the congregation of the righteous* (Ps 1:4-5).

Finally, the parallelism of verse six contrasts the lives of the righteous with the unrighteous. "To know" means to experience closeness in relationship because of being likeminded. On the day of judgment Yahushua will say to some believers, *"I never knew you. Away from me, you evildoers!"* (Mt 7:23). They were doing "good church works," but they had lost their relationship with Elohim.

> *For Yahuah knows the way of the righteous,*
> *But the way of the unrighteous perishes* (Ps 1:6).

In summary, Psalm 1 contrasts the righteous with the wicked and exalts Yahuah and his word. We see this theme continually throughout the book.

Psalm 13, a psalm of David, has a theme of being forsaken, yet trusting Elohim. Several psalms have this theme (see Ps 13:1,5).

Psalm 14, of David, has the theme of the wickedness of man.

> *The fool has said in his heart, "There is no Elohim."*
> *They have done corruptly,*
> *They have done an abominable deed,*
> *There is none who does good* (Ps 14:1).

Psalm 19, of David, extols Elohim in creation and in his word.

Psalm 22, of David, is an example of the many Messianic psalms; that is, psalms that are fulfilled in Yahushua Messiah. It begins with his words on the stake of being forsaken, but continues to show his trust in Yahuah.

Psalm 23, of David, is probably the most remembered of all the psalms.

> *Yahuah* is my shepherd;
> *I do not lack* (Ps 23:1).

> *Only goodness and kindness follow me*
> *All the days of my life,*
> *And I shall dwell in the house of Yahuah*
> *To the length of days! [forever]* (Ps 23:6).

Psalm 44 is an example of relating Elohim's deeds to bring his people into the Promised Land.

Psalm 47 is an example of praise.

Oh, clap your hands*, all you peoples!*
Shout to Elohim with a voice of singing! (Ps 47:1).

Psalm 51 is another example showing David's personal life. It is a prayer asking for forgiveness for his sin with Bathsheba.

Psalm 90 is a prayer of Moses the man of Elohim.

Psalm 110 is another Messianic psalm of David. Yahushua quoted this to show he was greater than David. It is also quoted in the book of Hebrews (Heb 7:21).

Yahuah said *to my master,*
"Sit at my right hand
Until I make your enemies your footstool" (Ps 110:1).

Yahuah has sworn *and does not relent,*
"You are a priest forever
According to the order of Melchizedek" (Ps 110:4).

Psalm 117 is the shortest psalm, and also the shortest "chapter" in the scriptures.

Praise Yahuah, all you nations!
Extol him, all you peoples!
For his kindness is mighty over us
And the truth of Yahuah is everlasting.
Hallu Yah (Praise Yah)! (Ps 117:1-2).

Psalm 119, with 176 verses, is the longest psalm. It is an acrostic poem. This means that each section begins with a letter of the Hebrew alphabet in consecutive order. It is a psalm showing how wonderful Yahuah and his word are. (See Ps 119:11, 18, 71, 105, 130.)

Psalm 126 is a song of ascents, having to do with worship in the temple.

Psalm 136 is an example of a chorus or refrain following a statement. It has 26 verses, and each concludes with the phrase *"For his kindness is forever."* Here is the first verse.

Give thanks to Yahuah for he is good!
For his kindness is forever (Ps 136:1).

Some psalms were written during the captivity in Babylon. Psalm 137 is one of them. This is also an imprecatory psalm; that is, it calls down evil upon the wicked. Here is the last verse.

Blissful is he who shall take
And dash your little ones against the rock (Ps 137:9).

This may sound unchristian, for we are to forgive our enemies. But this is prophetic of what indeed would happen. This is a prayer that the wicked be destroyed. We have seen throughout our survey already that sin results in judgment. So this is a prayer in agreement with Elohim's anger against wickedness. For us as believers in Messiah, the judgment we want to do is rescue souls from the enemy, Satan, who has taken them captive.

There are many precious sayings in the book of Psalms, too many to include in our short survey. This has only been a sampling.

3. Proverbs

PROVERBS AND ITS COMPANION BOOK ECCLESIASTES have been called Wisdom Literature, for they are full of sayings regarding wisdom in practical everyday living. This is in contrast to the book of Psalms which focuses on the spiritual side of things. We begin with comments from Easton's Bible Dictionary.

> PROVERBS, BOOK OF
> — a collection of moral and philosophical maxims of a wide range of subjects presented in a poetic form. ...
> This book is usually divided into three parts: (1.) Consisting of ch. 1-9, which contain an exhibition of wisdom as the highest good.
> (2.) Consisting of ch. 10-24.
> (3.) Containing proverbs of Solomon "which the men of Hezekiah, the king of Judah, collected" (ch. 25-29).
> These are followed by two supplements, (1) "The words of Agur" (ch. 30); and (2) "The words of king Lemuel" (ch. 31).
> Solomon is said to have written three thousand proverbs, and those contained in this book may be a selection from these (1 Kings 4:32). In the New Testament there are thirty-five direct quotations from this book or allusions to it.
> (Easton's Bible Dictionary)

The first seven verses prepare the way for understanding the whole book.

The proverbs of Solomon son of David, king of Israel:
To know wisdom and restraint,
   To distinguish words of understanding,
To receive the restraint of intelligence,
   Righteousness, judgment, and straightness;
To give discretion to the foolish,
   Knowledge and discernment to the young.
A wise one hears and increases learning,
   And one of understanding acquires wise counsel,
To understand a proverb and a figure,
   The words of the wise and their riddles.
The fear of Yahuah is the beginning of knowledge;
   Fools despise wisdom and restraint (Pr 1:1-7).

Look again at verse 6. Webster's Dictionary says this of the word "proverb" with respect to the Bible: "a profound saying, maxim, or oracular utterance *requiring interpretation*" (italics added). Some of the proverbs are easy to understand, but many require interpretation, and all require elaboration. Here are a few examples.

Who is simple? Let him turn in here.
   And as for him who lacks heart,
   She says to him,
      [She is a foolish woman, referring to the flesh nature]
"Stolen waters are sweet
   And bread eaten in secret is pleasant."
But he does not know that the dead are there,
   Her guests in the depths of Sheol (Pr 9:16-18).

"Sheol" is a Hebrew word meaning "place of the dead"; it means the same as the Greek word "Hades." This saying means the wicked are so stupid that they don't know their actions will take them to hell. The book of Proverbs is full of the consequences of sin and how stupid it is to yield to the flesh nature. Often there is a parallel of contrast.

A healing tongue is a tree of life,
   But perverseness in it ruins the spirit.
A fool despises his father's restraint,
   But he who heeds reproof is prudent (Pr 15:4-5).

110

Often also there is a parallel of result.

Commit your works to Yahuah,
And your plans shall be established (Pr 16:3).

When a man's ways please Yahuah,
He makes even his enemies to be at peace with him. (Pr 16:7).

Train up a child in the way he should go,
Even when he is old he will not turn away from it (Pr 22:6).

If you fail in the day of distress
Your strength is small! (Pr 24:10).

A little sleep, a little slumber,
A little folding of the hands to rest;
And your poverty shall come, a prowler,
And your need like an armed man (Pr 24:33-34).

Chapter 31:10-31 concludes the book of Proverbs with a description of the kind of bride Messiah is looking for (Pro 31:10, 26-29).

4. Ecclesiastes

Ecclesiastes is a companion book to Proverbs and is also part of the Wisdom Literature. It is a mixture of prose and poetry. Translators can tell by style which is which, and some show the poetry in their translations.

The name "Ecclesiastes" comes from the Septuagint translation of the Hebrew scriptures into Greek. The Hebrew name for it is Qoheleth, which means Teacher, or one who speaks to an assembly. A frequent phrase is *"under the sun."* This shows that the whole of Ecclesiastes is from the point of view of man of earth, not as Elohim sees things and how they are in the spirit.

"Emptiness! Emptiness!" says the Teacher.
"Emptiness, all is empty!"
What gain has man from all his labor
In which he toils under the sun? (Ecc 1:2-3).

And I set my heart to seek and search out by wisdom concerning all that has been done under the sky; this evil travail Elohim has given to the sons of man, to be humbled by it. 1:14 I

111

have seen all the works that are done under the sun. And behold, all is empty and vexation of spirit (Ecc 1:13).

Now all has been heard; here is the conclusion of the matter: Fear the Elohim and keep his commandments, for this is the whole duty of man (Ecc 12:13).

This conclusion is in the two greatest commandments—love Elohim with everything within you, and love your neighbor as yourself.

For Elohim will bring into judgment every deed, including every hidden thing, whether good or whether evil (Ecc 12:14).

The good deeds are deeds done in loving Elohim, not what man considers good. The evil deeds include what man thinks is good.

If the last two verses of the book (Ecc 12:13-14) had not been included, then this book would be very pessimistic and wouldn't have been included among the inspired collection. It is the closing verses that give meaning to all that precedes. They are the guiding principle for understanding the book. The book teaches that nothing in this life has any lasting value. To the man of the world, this life is all there is, and so a person must work for his own enjoyment. And we do find it to be true that among them there are those who seem to be happy and content with this life. The lukewarm believer in Messiah is not much different. He believes intellectually that Elohim is the source of eternal life and happiness, but he lives his life focused on the things of this world. The thinking of both categories results in the same, for it is the mind of the flesh nature. The apostle Paul wrote about this problem.

"For being flesh-minded is death, but spirit-minded is life and peace" (Ro 8:6).

The Teacher (author of the book) is speaking from the point of view of being spirit-minded. The closer a believer gets to Yahuah in intimate fellowship, the more the believer realizes how empty life is without him. But when one *is* in fellowship with Yahuah, he can go through *"this evil travail Elohim has given to the sons of man"* (the work-a-day world), recognizing that these hardships are only temporary and they work for our benefit.

"We know that for those who love Elohim all things work together for good, those who are called according to his purpose" (Ro 8:28).

The book of Ecclesiastes goes through every category of life to show how futile life is without Elohim. At times the book also speaks from the point of view of the world.

In this survey of the book we can only point out a few things. But the point of view is important, because it helps us understand why the Teacher says everything is futile, or meaningless, or vanity, or empty (depending on the translation).

Although life is meaningless apart from Elohim, in whatever activity a person is doing, the Teacher gives practical advice in how to make the best of it. (See Ecc 7:5; 8:14-15.)

The following selection about the dead knowing nothing (Ecc 9:5-6) needs a comment. This is one of the passages used by those who teach a doctrine called "soul sleep," that when a person's body dies, his soul sleeps until the resurrection for judgment, so he knows nothing until that time. But this passage teaches no such thing. The perspective is what it appears like to those who are living *"under the sun."* That is the subject, not life or existence after death.

Here are two verses of wisdom regarding practical life.

In the morning sow your seed and until evening do not let your hand rest, since you do not know which shall prosper, this or that, or whether both alike are good (Ecc 11:6).

Remember also your creator in the days of your youth before the evil days come and the years draw near when you say, "I have no pleasure in them" (Ecc 12:1).

See again the last two verses of Ecclesiastes (Ecc 12:13-14).

Much can be learned from this book, for it contains many practical truths, truths which are confirmed in other scriptures, the book of Proverbs being one of them.

5. Song of Songs

HERE IS A RIDDLE to begin our survey of Song of Songs.

Virginity led to the death of a prince.
Old age led to the romance of a king.

The key to this riddle is Abishag from Shunem. We learned of her in First Kings chapter 1. She was selected in a beauty contest to be wife to King David in order to warm him in his old age. When he died, she became a widow while still a virgin. When Solomon succeeded David as king (and therefore inherited Abishag as a wife) his half-brother Adonijah asked for Abishag, which resulted in his execution for treason.

Because Adonijah was a son of David, he was a prince: *"Virginity led to the death of a prince."* Because of his old age, David never "knew" Abishag, and so Solomon inherited a beautiful, young virgin as a wife. The Song of Songs is a love poem showing the romance of King Solomon with Abishag. He wanted her love, a totally devoted love, before taking her as wife: *"Old age led to the romance of a king."*

This riddle is not found in scripture, nor is this an interpretation of Song of Songs. Scriptures do not relate any relationship between Solomon and Abishag, one way or another. The woman in this Song who is the beloved of Solomon is not given a name, only that she is from Shulam, a town of which we have no record.

Some believe that, for the purposes of the Song, the place of her birth was changed into a spiritual place that does not exist in the natural realm, a name that matched that of Solomon, because the two would become one in marriage. In the Song we see that the Shulammite matches what was likely the life of Abishag before she came to the palace. The name Solomon and the name Shulam both come from the word *"shalom,"* which means "completeness, soundness, welfare, peace" (Strong's # 7965).

The Song is a conversation between Solomon and his beloved in poetic form that can be likened to an allegory. Occasionally a chorus speaks.

> An allegory is a representation of an abstract or spiritual meaning through concrete or material forms; figurative treatment of one subject under the guise of another. (Webster)

The conversations tell how much they love each other, sometimes in rather amorous language. Keep in mind, however, that marriage and intimacy were created to be a type of spiritual marriage and intimacy with Messiah. In this Song, Solomon is a type of Messiah, and the Shulamite is a type of the bride company of believers. As one reads through the Song, he sees a progression of maturity in the bride. The Song is full of typology, but for our survey purposes we will look at a few lines to see the progression.

The bride speaking:

> *"Do not look upon me, because I am dark,*
> *Because the sun has looked on me"* (SS 1:6).

Abishag was a girl who worked in the fields in the sun before being chosen. That's why she was dark. Those in the palace stay out of the sun, so they are lighter. Those from the Middle East naturally have a darker complexion than those from northern Europe, and in the sun they become very dark. Her darkness is a type of a new believer who still has some darkness inside to overcome.

The bride speaking:

> *Now let me arise and go about the city,*
> *In the streets and in the broad places.*
> *I seek him whom my soul loves.*
> *I sought him, but I did not find him"* (SS 3:2).

This is speaking spiritually, for in the natural Abishag would not be going about the city to look for Solomon. In our spiritual lives, Messiah sometimes comes close so that we feel his presence, and sometimes draws away so that we will put effort into seeking him.

Solomon speaking:

> *"Your neck is like the tower of David*
> *Built for an armory,*
> *On which hang a thousand shields,*
> *All armor of mighty men"* (SS 4:4).

This is part of Solomon's song to the bride telling her how beautiful and wonderful she is. In this verse he is comparing her to an army; in type, that she is the warrior bride. In the last days, the bride of Messiah will rise up in mighty power to do even greater miracles than Yahushua did.

The bride speaking:

> "I was sleeping but my heart was awake –
>   The voice of my beloved! He knocks,
>   Open for me, my sister, my love,
>   My dove, my perfect one;
>   For my head is drenched with dew,
>   My locks with the drops of the night' (SS 5:2).

> "I opened for my beloved,
>   But my beloved had turned away, had gone.
>   My being went out when he spoke.
>   I sought him but I could not find him;
>   I called him but he gave me no answer" (SS 5:6).

In type, the bride is still maturing, but also still spiritually asleep. So Messiah calls, then withdraws himself so that she will seek all the harder. And she does. By the end of the Song she finally has given herself totally to him, and he cannot bear to be away from her.

The bride speaking:

> "Hurry, my beloved,
>   And be like a gazelle or a young stag
>   On the mountains of spices" (SS 8:14).

This is the last verse of the Song. In type, Messiah has ascended to the Father and has been given all authority in heaven and earth. And the assembly bride is eager for his return.

> *He that bears witness of these things says, "Yes, I am coming speedily." Amen. Yes, come, Master Yahushua!* (Rev 22:20).

FIVE MAJOR PROPHETS

THE TERM "MAJOR PROPHETS" refers to those prophets whose books are the longest. They are given in chronological order according to when they were written. All the prophets have the message of repent so as to avoid judgment, but judgment will indeed come because the people won't repent. But there is hope, because a remnant will repent and receive the blessings of Yahuah.

All the writing prophets, the five major and the twelve minor, use some poetry in their writing.

1. Isaiah

ISAIAH IN HEBREW is Yeshayahu. The name combines two words, "salvation" and "Yahuah." It has the same meaning as Yahushua (Jesus, Joshua), with the words in reverse order. It can mean "Yahuah has saved," or "Yahuah is salvation." This is the way it is with Hebrew names: to translate into English, one has to add the connecting verb and choose the form (noun or verb) to convey the idea in a sentence. In Hebrew thinking there is no need to make a sentence; all that is needed is the root words in the name: "salvation Yahuah."

Isaiah, the author of this book, was probably born in Jerusalem of a family related to the royal house of Judah. He was an official of King Uzziah of Judah (2Ch 26:22), and when the king died (740 B.C.) he received a vision from Elohim in which he was called to be a prophet Is 6). He was married to a woman described as "the prophetess" (Is 8:3) and had two sons whom they named Shear-Jashub ("a remnant shall return") (Is 7:3), and Maher-Shalal-Hash-Baz ("Speed the Spoil, Hasten the Booty" (Is 8:3). These names show the two basic themes of the book: Elohim is about to bring judgment upon his people, therefore Maher-Shalal-Hash-Baz ("Speed the Spoil, Hasten the Booty), but afterwards there will be an outpouring of Elohim's mercy and favor to the remnant of people who will remain faithful to him, therefore Shear-Jashub ("a remnant shall return").

Yahuah told Isaiah that most of his ministry would be about judgment. Even though he would speak the truth, the people would reject it (Is 6:10). Yahushua quoted from Isaiah about his own ministry (Mt 13:14-15). Yahuah further told Isaiah that the Babylonians would devastate Judah (the southern kingdom) and take the people into exile. This happened in 587/586 B.C.

> *Then I said, "Adonai, how long?" And he answered,*
> *"Until cities are waisted and without inhabitant,*
> *And houses are without people*
> *And the land is utterly desolate,*
> *"And Yahuah has removed men far away*

> *And the forsaken places are many in the midst*
>   *of the land.*
> *"Yet there will be a tenth portion in it,*
>   *And it will again be subject to burning,*
>   *Like a terebinth or an oak*
>   *Whose stump remains when it is felled.*
>   *The set-apart seed is its stump"* (Is 6:11-13).

According to Jewish tradition, Isaiah was martyred during the reign of the wicked king Manasseh of Judah by being placed in a hollow log and sawn in half. This may be what the book of Hebrews meant when speaking of the heroes of faith, that some were sawn in two (Heb 11:37).

With this general introduction in mind here are a few passages.

> *"Come now and let us reason together," Says Yahuah.*
>   *"Though your sins are like scarlet,*
>   *They shall be as white as snow;*
>   *Though they are red like crimson,*
>   *They shall be as wool.*
> *"If you are willing and obedient,*
>   *You shall eat the good of the land;*
> *"But if you refuse and rebel,*
>   *You shall be devoured by the sword,"*
>   *For the mouth of Yahuah has spoken* (Is 1:18-20)..

The above passage is an appeal to repentance, the result if there is repentance, and the result if they don't repent. It follows a list of the many evils Judah was involved in, and following it is a similar list. This is a recurring theme throughout the whole of Isaiah.

> *"And I shall turn my hand against you*
>   *And shall refine your dross as with lye*
>   *And shall remove all your alloy.*
> *"And I shall give back your judges as at the first*
>   *And your counselors as at the beginning.*
>   *After this you shall be called the city of righteousness,*
>   *A faithful city"* (Is 1:25-26).

The above passage is also a recurring theme. The judgment that will come will result in a remnant that will repent and truly follow

Yahuah. This will happen in the Millennium after Messiah's return.

> *In that day the Branch of Yahuah shall be splendid and esteemed. And the fruit of the earth shall be excellent and beautiful for the escaped ones of Israel* (Is 4:2).

"*In that day*" refers to the Millennium. This introduces a Messianic title. Yahushua is called "the Branch of Yahuah."

> *And he shall lift up a banner to the nations from afar*
> *And shall whistle to them from the end of the earth* (Is 5:26).

"*The nations from afar*" refers to Yahuah calling Babylon to be the instrument of judgment upon Judah. The final fulfillment of this will be the Battle of Armageddon, in which all the nations of the world with a united army attack Jerusalem.

Isaiah 6:1-10 records Yahuah's call to Isaiah to be a prophet to his people. In a vision Isaiah sees Adonai in great esteem. "Adonai" is a Hebrew word that means "master." It is a title for Yahuah, but it also applies to his Son Yahushua, for all that Yahushua did was a reflection of his Father. That is why Yahushua said to Philip, "*Anyone who has seen me has seen the Father*" (John 14:9). (See Jn 12:36-41.)

So in this vision Isaiah was seeing the future Messiah in his esteemed position of having received all authority from Yahuah, the Father.

> *And I heard the voice of Adonai, saying, "Whom do I send and who would go for us?" And I said, "Behold! I! Send me"* (Is 6:8).

The "Us" in this passage refers to Yahuah (the one speaking), to his messengers (angels created to help us, Heb. 1:14), to his future Son Yahushua, and to Yahuah's people throughout all the ages who want to love Yahuah with all their heart, soul, mind and strength. For us today, he is speaking to the bride assembly.

Isaiah 7:1-16 records an event in the life of Ahaz king of Judah. The kings of Israel and Aram (Syria) plotted together to come against Judah to destroy it. When Ahaz became afraid, Yahuah told him (through Isaiah) not to worry, for in 65 years Israel (the northern kingdom) would be a nation no more. Then Yahuah gave Ahaz a sign that this would happen, a sign that had a double fulfillment.

> "*Therefore Adonai himself gives you a sign: Behold, the*

maiden conceives and bears a son and she shall call his name Immanuel. [cp. Mt 1:23.] *He eats cheese and honey when he knows to refuse the evil and choose the good* (when he is old enough to know right from wrong). *For before the child knows to refuse evil and choose the good, the land that you dread* [Israel and Syria] *is to be forsaken by both her kings* (Is 7:14-16)..

The first fulfillment of this prophecy was a few years later; that is, the length of time from conception to the baby being old enough to know right from wrong. It happened when Assyria conquered both Syria and Israel. The final fulfillment was the birth of Yahushua Messiah. (See Is 9:6-7 and 11:1-2 for two more familiar Messianic prophecies.)

The Book of Revelation speaks of the seven spirits of Elohim (Rev 1:5; 3:1; 4:5; 5:6). This refers to the seven-fold aspect of Elohim's spirit. In a prophecy about the coming Messiah, Isaiah says what those seven spirits are.

> *Spirit of Yahuah will rest on him,*
>> *Spirit of wisdom and understanding,*
>> *Spirit of counsel and strength,*
>> *Spirit of knowledge and the fear of Yahuah* (Is 11:2).
> (The Hebrew has no article "the" with spirit in this verse.)

These are what we Messianans should be seeking to have also.

Isaiah pronounced many judgments on the nations around Israel, with many against Babylon, for Babylon represents all that is evil in the world. *"Babylon is fallen, is fallen"* (Is 21:9). The repeat of "is fallen" emphasizes that her doom is certain. (Rev 14:8 and 18:2 also speaks of this.)

Isaiah 38-39 records Hezekiah's sickness, prayer and healing. Yahuah told him (through Isaiah) that his sickness would lead to death. Hezekiah prayed that he was too young to die, and appealed to his "perfect heart." So Yahuah added 15 years to his life and gave a sign. He brought the shadow on the sundial ten degrees backward (Is 38:8). (Other translations have stairway and steps instead of sundial and degrees.)

Ahaz, a wicked king of Judah, was the father of Hezekiah. After Hezekiah recovered from his sickness, ambassadors came from Babylon to congratulate him on his recovery, and Hezekiah showed them all the treasures in his treasure room. Because of that, Yahuah told him (through Isaiah) that all the treasures would be taken away to

Babylon along with exiles, but not in his lifetime.

There are many passages in Isaiah in which Yahuah declares that he alone is Elohim; there is no other (Is 43:10-11; 44:6; 45:5-7).

The last section of Isaiah has many prophecies about the restoration of Israel, all of which apply to the Millennium. They are given to reassure Israel that judgment was given for a reason, and afterwards there will be restoration (Is 51:3,11).

Perhaps the most well known of the Messianic prophecies is Isaiah 53, for in it we see described the suffering and death of Yahushua for our sins.

> *We all, like sheep, went astray;*
> *Each one has turned to his own way.*
> *And Yahuah has laid on him the iniquity of us all* (Is 53:6).

A question regarding the righteous dying is answered in the following verse.

> *The righteous one perished and no one takes it to heart.*
> *And kind men are taken away while no one understands*
> *That the righteous one is taken away from the evil* (Is 57:1).

Besides being a general principle, it also applies to the rapture of the bride before the great tribulation.

This survey of Isaiah closes with references to some verses that show the kind of people Yahuah is looking for: people who are the reason for creation, who will live forever with him in his eternal kingdom on the new earth as the bride of Messiah (Is 57:15; 66:1-2).

> *"But to this one I will look,*
> *To him who is humble and contrite of spirit*
> *And who trembles at my word"* (Is 66:2).

Great are the depths of spiritual meanings contained in this book. This has only been a sampling of the many treasures contained in it.

2. Jeremiah

JEREMIAH IN HEBREW is Yirmeyah or Yirmeyahu (yir-meh-YAH or yir-meh-YAH-hoo). (Whenever "-iah" is the ending of a name, in Hebrew it is either "yah" or "yahu," the name of Yahuah). As with Isaiah (Yeshayahu) it is a combination of two words, "appointed" and "Yahuah." Together it means "raised up or appointed by Yahuah." He is the second of the writing prophets.

By the time of Jeremiah, Israel (the northern kingdom) is gone. The people had been taken captive and dispersed by the Assyrian Empire, and only Judah (the southern kingdom) is left. As with the other prophets, this one warns of judgment on Judah because of their sin, and also promises restoration after they have repented and turned from their evil ways.

Jeremiah is known as "the weeping prophet" because of his emotional agony over the sins of his nation.

> *Oh, that my head were waters*
> > *And my eyes a fountain of tears,*
> > *And I would weep day and night*
> > *For the slain of the daughter of my people!* (Jer 9:1).

In this respect he is a type of Yahushua Messiah who cried:

> *"Jerusalem, Jerusalem, killing the prophets and stoning those who are sent to her! How often I wished to gather your children together the way a hen gathers her chickens under her wings, but you would not!* 38 *Look! Your house is left to you a waste"* (Mt 23:37).

Jeremiah's prophecies are not recorded in the order of time, and they have frequent repetitions. Yet the people would not believe the warnings. Isaiah, over a hundred years earlier, said:

> *But the word of Yahuah was to them,*
> > *"Command upon command, command upon command,*
> > *Line upon line, line upon line,*
> > *A little here, a little there,"*
> > *So that they go and shall stumble backward*
> > *And be broken and snared and taken* (Is 28:13).

Jeremiah has several Messianic prophecies. Two of them speak of David being a Branch of righteousness (Jer 23:5-6; 33:15-17).

A repeated message throughout the scriptures is judgment for sin and restoration of a remnant who repent and obey Yahuah. Some examples of this are:

- At the time of Noah billions of people were judged by the flood, and only a remnant of eight saved.

- Most of the Hebrews who left Egypt died in the wilderness, and only a remnant entered the Promised Land.
- At the time of Jeremiah the people of Judah were taken captive to Babylon, and only a remnant returned after 70 years.
- Jerusalem was destroyed after the Jews rejected Messiah (at which time the Gentile church age began), and (after the church age is over) only a remnant will be saved when Messiah returns to establish his 1000-year rule on earth.

The last three examples refer to the nation of Israel, for they are the covenant people of Yahuah.

This pattern applies to the gentile church age as well. The gentile church age is between Messiah's rejection by Israel and his return, a period of about 2,000 years. Regarding what happened in the history of Israel, which includes the book of Jeremiah, Paul wrote:

"And all these came upon them as examples, and they were written as a warning to us upon whom the ends of the ages have come" (1Cor 10:11).

The gentile assembly began pure at Pentecost, but quickly became just as corrupt as Judah was at the time of Jeremiah. So the warnings to repent or be destroyed apply to the assembly today. Likewise, their destruction because of refusal to repent also applies to the assembly today. That is to say, the vast majority of the assembly today will refuse to repent, because they love their corrupt traditions.

We are near the end of the gentile assembly age when the attention of Yahuah will again be upon Israel. Four events mark that end:

- The rise of world government with the antichrist being the ruler.
- The 3½ -years male-son/warrior-bride ministry of Rev. 12:1-11.
- The rapture of the bride of Messiah at the end of that ministry, the bride being a small minority of the assembly.
- The 3½ -years "great tribulation" upon the rest of the assembly, in which those who repent will be killed for their faith.

A short time after the last gentile believer is martyred, Yahuah judges the nations with plagues that last for 3½ years. The last plague is the return of Messiah that ends the Battle of Armageddon and begins his 1,000-year rule, called the Millennium. The promises of restoration to Israel in the book of Jeremiah (and the other prophetic books) will have their fulfillment in the Millennium, for it is only during the last plague that Israel (only a remnant) repents and believes in him whom they pierced.

This is the pattern we see in the book of Jeremiah:

- Israel is called to repent because of their wickedness and idolatry.
- They refuse to repent.
- Babylon destroys their city and takes them captive.
- Israel is restored.
- Babylon and the nations are destroyed. Babylon is a type of the last-day world government.

Some of the above comments have been given before, but repetition is good. It helps us see the book of Jeremiah in light of the whole picture.

Chapter 1:1-10 records the call of Jeremiah. It came during the reign of Josiah, the last righteous king of Judah.

> *Now the word of Yahuah came to me, saying,*
> *"Before I formed you in the belly I knew you,*
> *And before you came out of the womb I set you apart.*
> *I appointed you a prophet to nations"* (Jer 1:4-5).

As with Moses many years before, Jeremiah didn't want the job. He complained that he was still a youth and didn't know how to speak.

> *But Yahuah said to me,*
> *"Do not say, 'I am a youth,'*
> *But go to all to whom I send you*
> *And speak whatever I command you.*
> *"Do not fear their faces,*
> *For I am with you to deliver you," declares Yahuah.*
> *Then Yahuah put forth his hand and touched my mouth,*
> *And Yahuah said to me,*
> *"See, I have put my words in your mouth.*
> *"Behold, I have this day set you over the nations*
> *   and over the kingdoms,*
> *"To root out and to pull down,*
> *"To destroy and to overthrow,*
> *"To build and to plant"* (Jer 1:7-10).

It was the words of Yahuah through Jeremiah that would do the overthrowing and building. Jeremiah would speak it, and Yahuah would do it.

Jeremiah had two visions. In the first he saw a branch of an almond tree. The word for almond tree also means watching. By this vision Yahuah was telling Jeremiah that he was watching over his word to do it (Jer 1:11-12). This would give assurance to Jeremiah.

In the second vision he saw a boiling pot that was facing away from the north. This was showing that Yahuah's judgment on Judah was coming from the north; that is, from Babylon in the east, but having to come to Judah by way of the Euphrates River, which was in the north (Jer 1:13-16).

Then follows the charges of wickedness that Yahuah has against Judah, and that's why they deserve judgment. One charge was that they had seen the judgment that came on Israel because of their sin, yet not only did Judah not repent, but did even worse than Israel did (Jer 3:6-11).

Promises of restoration and honor are interspersed between the denunciations on Judah for their sin and calls to repentance. These promises will be fulfilled during the Millennium.

> *"At that time Jerusalem shall be called the throne of Yahuah, and all the nations shall be gathered to it, to the name of Yahuah to Jerusalem, and no longer walk after the stubbornness of their evil heart"* (Jer 3:17).

The wickedness in Judah had gotten so bad that Yahuah told Jeremiah not to pray for this people, for he won't hear (Jer 7:16). But Jeremiah loved the people, and because of that love he wept for them (Jer 9:1). What Yahuah wants from his people is that they don't boast in their riches, but that they boast in understanding and knowing him, that he is doing kindness and justice in the earth, for he delights in this (Jer 9:23-24).

Chapter 11:18-23 records that the men of Anathoth, Jeremiah's home town, promised that if he didn't stop his prophesying they would kill him. In response, Yahuah told Jeremiah that those men and their families would die by the sword and famine.

When Jeremiah complained about the workers of treachery being at ease as compared to the righteous such as himself, Yahuah gave this encouragement: (Notice the parallelism in this poetry.)

125

"If you have run with the footmen,
  And they have wearied you,
    [i.e. your present small trials]
  Then how do you contend with horses?
    [when trials will be worse]*?*
And if in the land of peace in which you trusted
  They wearied you,
  Then how do you manage in the Jordan thicket?
    [or, in its annual flood stage] (Jer 12:5).

In his book Jeremiah reveals his emotional battles in the ministry, so it is easy to identify with him.

Chapter 13:1-14 records two prophetic object lessons. In the first, Jeremiah put on a linen sash, then hid it in a hole by the Euphrates river and later dug it up. When it was dug up, it was ruined, completely useless. This was a sign that Yahuah would ruin the pride of Jerusalem.

In the second object lesson Jeremiah told the people that every wineskin should be filled with wine. That puzzled them, for they knew that. Then came the object lesson. All the inhabitants of the land, from high rank to low, would be filled with drunkenness and be destroyed.

In chapter 15 Jeremiah makes an appeal to Yahuah wanting vengeance on those who are persecuting him. Also he asked not to be killed. He was suffering reproach on account of the message Yahuah gave him. In response Yahuah told him to repent of his self-pity, and then he can be useful as a prophet (Jer 15:15-18).

In chapter 16 we have an interesting prophecy regarding the end times and the Millennium after true repentance: *"And they shall know that my name is Yahuah!"* (Jer 16:21). We are in the days in which Yahuah is revealing his name, and also the name of his Son, Yahushua.

One of the last kings in Judah was Coniah (also called Jehoiachin). Because of his wickedness, a curse was put upon him that none of his descendents would become a king (Jer 22:30). He did have children, but none of his descendents would inherit the throne or be in the Messianic line. In the Matthew genealogy he is in the lineage of Joseph, his legal father, but he is not in the genealogy recorded in Luke.

Jeremiah prophesied that the captivity in Babylon would last for seventy years, and then a remnant would return to Jerusalem (Jer 25:11-12; 29:10-14). The latter part of this prophecy will be fulfilled in the Millennium:

> *"And you shall seek me and shall find me when you search for me with all your heart, and I shall be found by you," declares Yahuah. "And I shall turn back your captivity and shall gather you from all the nations and from all the places where I have driven you," declares Yahuah. "And I shall bring you back to the place from where I have exiled you"* (Jer 29:13-14).

There were three deportations of the people to Babylon before Jerusalem was totally destroyed. Throughout that time Yahuah told the people, through Jeremiah, that if they would surrender, then all would be well with them and Yahuah would bless them, but if they did not, they would die by sword, famine and pestilence. But the rulers called this treason, and Jeremiah was imprisoned several times, one time in a cistern in which he sank in the mud.

Babylon would not have destroyed Jerusalem if the people would have submitted. But they wouldn't. They trusted that because they had the temple, Yahuah would protect them. But it is only through obedience to Yahuah that one gets protection.

In the final deportation Jeremiah was given permission to stay with the remnant of the poor people left in the land, or to go to Babylon. Jeremiah chose to stay. Babylon appointed Gedaliah as governor of Judah, but he was soon assassinated, and the people feared retribution from Babylon and wanted to go to Egypt to be safe. Jeremiah told them not to flee, and if they did, Babylon would pursue them and destroy them in Egypt. Again, the people didn't believe him and forced Jeremiah to go with them. When they got to Egypt, Jeremiah told them they would be consumed by the sword and hunger until they are no more (Jer 44:26-28). And so it happened. Babylon conquered Egypt and killed or took into exile most of those who had escaped to Egypt.

Chapters 46-51 contain prophecies of judgment against the gentile nations. Some of them would be annihilated never to recover as a nation, but some were promised that they would be restored.

In Jeremiah there is much repetition regarding judgment on Judah and restoration in the Millennium, there are stories of Jeremiah's persecution, and there are judgments on the nations.

Next we look at Jeremiah's lament over what happened to Judah and Jerusalem.

3. Lamentations

Easton's BIBLE DICTIONARY gives a good summary.

Called in the Hebrew canon *'Ekhah*, meaning "How," being the formula for the commencement of a song of wailing. It is the first word of the book (see 2Sa.1:19-27). The LXX [Greek Septuagint translation] adopted the name rendered "Lamentations" (Gr. *threnoi* = Heb. *qinoth*) now in common use, to denote the character of the book, in which the prophet mourns over the desolations brought on the city and the holy land by Chaldeans.

The book consists of five separate poems.

In Lam. 1 the prophet dwells on the manifold miseries oppressed by which the city sits as a solitary widow weeping sorely.

In Lam. 2 these miseries are described in connection with the national sins that had caused them.

Lam. 3 speaks of hope for the people of God. The chastisement would only be for their good; a better day would dawn for them.

Lam. 4 laments the ruin and desolation that had come upon the city and temple, but traces it only to the people's sins.

Lam. 5 is a prayer that Zion's reproach may be taken away in the repentance and recovery of the people.

The first four poems (chapters) are acrostics, like some of the Psalms (Ps. 25, 34, 37, 119), i.e., each verse begins with a letter of the Hebrew alphabet taken in order. The first, second, and fourth have each twenty-two verses, the number of the letters in the Hebrew alphabet. The third has sixty-six verses, in which each three successive verses begin with the same letter. The fifth is not acrostic.

(Easton's Bible Dictionary)

Look up and read these key verses: (Lam 1:3,5; 2:17-18; 3:21-23,31-33; 4:10; 5:21-22). Verse 4:10 speaks of women boiling and eating their own children. This happened literally during the siege. Likely the child had died first of starvation.

4. Ezekiel

EZEKIEL IN HEBREW is Yᵉḥezqĕl (pronounced yeh-khehz-KAIL). It is a combination of two words: Yᵉḥezq (strengthened) and ĕl (the shortened form of Elohim), so "strengthened of Elohim."

> DATE WRITTEN: Probably recorded over the 22 year ministry of the prophet and completed around 565 B.C.
>
> PURPOSE: To relate a sovereign, holy God's condemnation of sinful ways and His continuing efforts to restore His people. He wants them to know that He is the Lord [that he is Yahuah].
>
> TO WHOM WRITTEN: Jewish exiles in Babylon and God's people everywhere.
>
> —Thompson Chain - Bible Book Outlines

Of special interest is Ezekiel's vision of the four living beings and Yahuah's commission to him in chapters 1- 3:14. These living beings come in a whirlwind from the north. This means they represent judgment, and that judgment would be from Babylon. The details of their appearance are not within the scope of this survey. They carried a throne above them on which was someone that had the appearance of a man and of the esteem of Yahuah. (Read especially Eze 2:3,9-10; 3:1,10-11,17.)

Notice that Ezekiel is called "son of man." This is because he is a human, he is representing humans, and he is pronouncing judgments to humans. In this way he is a type of Messiah. We see also from this that those who had gone into exile were still rebellious.

Chapters 4 and 5 record four signs Ezekiel did, signs with physical activity that would depict judgment. The idea is that although they refused to hear with their ears, they might hear with their eyes.

The first sign was acting out the siege of Jerusalem. He took a clay tablet, wrote on it the city of Jerusalem, built a siege wall against it, then put an iron plate between him and the city and set his face against it. This showed that Jerusalem would be attacked and Yahuah was against them.

The next two signs were to lie on his side for 390 days and to eat defiled bread during that time. In America you can buy bread called "Ezekiel's bread," so called from this event and the recipe for the bread. It is considered a health food bread and is expensive. However, this was a poor man's bread, something to make because of starvation and good ingredients were not available. Also it was to be baked over human dung, which would defile it. (Ezekiel got permission to use animal dung for baking so he wouldn't defile himself.) The purpose of this sign was to show how horrible it would be for the people of Jerusalem during the coming Babylonian siege.

The fourth sign was to use a sword to shave his head and beard and divide the hair into three parts, doing various things to it (Eze 5:2-4). The meaning of this sign is that one third of the people in Jerusalem would die of pestilence and famine, one third be killed by the sword, and one third scattered, and they shall know that Yahuah had spoken it (Eze 5:12-13).

The phrase *"And they shall know that I, Yahuah"* is used frequently in Ezekiel. When judgment comes they will know it came from Yahuah and that it was because of their sin.

Chapters 8-11 record a vision in which Ezekiel saw himself taken to Jerusalem to see the idolatry that was going on there, and the judgment that would result from their idolatry, and eventual restoration (Eze 8:3). He saw an image of jealousy, which was likely an obelisk, which is a phallic symbol for the worship of Baal. (Steeples on churches come from this practice.) He also saw carved images on the walls, women weeping for Tammuz, and elders facing the east in sun worship. (The Easter sunrise service comes from this practice.)

In the vision, a man clothed with linen went through the city and *"put a mark on the foreheads of the men who sigh and cry over all the abominations done in it"* (Eze 9:4).

Then six other men went throughout the city and killed all who didn't have the mark. But a surviving remnant is promised (Eze 11:17-21).

Chapter 16 records a parable of Israel's marriage with Yahuah. An abandoned newborn girl was rescued by Yahuah and raised by him to become a beautiful woman ready for marriage. But instead of marrying him, she gave herself as a prostitute to other nations and followed their wicked pagan practices. So Yahuah rejected her (Eze 16:59-60).

Chapter 18 is about personal judgment for personal sin. If a person sins, he dies for it. But if he repents, he will be forgiven and his sins will no longer be remembered. The reverse is also true. If a righteous person turns from his righteousness and sins and does not repent, then none of his righteousness will be remembered, and he will die for his sins. Further, no one is judged for the sin of his parents, nor is anyone rewarded for the righteousness of his parents.

"*The soul that is sinning shall die*" (Eze 18:4).

After pronouncing judgment on Judah, its leaders, its prophets and its people, Ezekiel also pronounces judgment on the various nations around, just as Isaiah and Jeremiah had done. There is one interesting judgment to look at, and that is the lamentation in chapter 27 for Tyre, a sea-merchant city-state on the Mediterranean. This one is interesting because it is a type of world government. And chapter 28:1-19 goes on further to lament over the king of Tyre. He is a type of Satan, who fell because of pride.

"*You were perfect in your ways*
From the day you were created
Until unrighteousness was found in you" (Eze 28:15).

In chapter 37 we have the vision in which Ezekiel saw a valley filled with very dry bones, and was told to prophesy for them to live. When he prophesied, the spirit came into them, they lived, and they stood on their feet, a very great army (Eze 37:10).

This was a prophecy of the restoration of the whole nation of Israel, Ephraim (the northern 10 tribes) and Judah (the southern two tribes). Following this prophecy, in chapters 38-39, we have a remarkable prophecy of the end-time battle of Armageddon in which Gog and Magog with a coalition of other nations come against the nation of Israel. Gog and Magog refer to Russia.

The rest of the book of Ezekiel (chs. 40-48) is a vision of the new temple in the Millennium, giving detailed dimensions, offerings, and worship, of the boundaries of the returned tribes of Israel, and of the new city Jerusalem. The book concludes with these words:

And the name of the city from that day is: Yahuah is there!
[Yahuah-shammah] (Eze 48:35).

Yahuah will be permanently with Israel in the Millennium because they no longer will backslide and go into idolatry. And in the Millennium, Israel will be the top nation of the world with Yahushua Messiah as the king over all the earth. Yahuah knew this before ever he created the earth, and he arranged that it would take 6,000 years to form them into a nation and get them to this place of loving obedience. The finished product is what he sees the whole time. He is that patient and loving. And he is that patient and loving toward us, knowing what each of us will be like when we individually become the finished product.

Regarding the assembly age, from Pentecost to the rapture, Yahuah arranged that it would take 2,000 years to get his assembly to be the mature bride of Messiah.

5. Daniel

DANIEL IN HEBREW is Dani'ĕl (pronounced dah-nee-AIL). It is a combination of three words: Dan (judge), i (a suffix meaning "my"), and ĕl (the shortened form of Elohim), so "my judge is Elohim," or "judgment of Elohim." The book is about judgment on Israel and the nations and about prophecies of the end times. It shows that Elohim is in charge of history.

The first seven chapters are chiefly history, and the rest chiefly prophecy. In the history part we see Daniel introduced and stories about Daniel and his three friends while in captivity among the Babylonians and Persians. They were taken captive by Babylon in one of the three groups of exiles from Judah from 597 to 581 BCE (Wikipedia). They were made eunuchs and trained to serve in the king's court.

When Daniel was given food as part of his preparation to serve the king, because the food was ceremonially unclean according to the Torah, he asked permission from the chief eunuch not to defile himself, and Elohim granted him kindness and compassion from the chief eunuch (Dan 1:8). In type, this is the bride not willing to contaminate herself with the pleasures of this world.

The first dream of King Nebuchadnezzar that Daniel interpreted was of a great image, representing the present and future kingdoms. The head of gold represented Babylon, the chest and arms of silver Medo-Persia, the legs of iron Rome, and its feet with mixed iron and clay the future antichrist government. The stone cut without hands that destroyed the image on its feet of iron and clay breaking them in pieces represents Messiah at his second coming destroying the antichrist one-world government (Dan 2:32-34).

In chapter 3 Nebuchadnezzar made a gold image that everyone was required to bow to. The penalty for refusal was to be thrown into a fiery furnace. Daniel's three friends, Shadrach, Meshach and Abednego, refused to obey, even though it meant their death (Dan 3:17-18). However, when they were thrown in they were not harmed.

After Nebuchadnezzar died, his son Belshazzar became king, and during a feast he saw a hand writing something on the wall, and he sent for Daniel to interpret it. The interpretation was that the king's reign was numbered, he was found lacking, and his kingdom would be given to the Medes and Persians (Dan 5:26-31). And so it happened that very night.

When Daniel was elevated in position, the governors of the provinces were jealous and wanted to destroy him. Because they could find no moral accusation against him, they went after his faith in Elohim. They convinced Darius to make a decree in which no one could petition any god for thirty days except the king himself, and punishment for disobedience was to be thrown into the den of lions. Daniel's response was to pray three times a day and give thanks before his Elah (Aramaic for Elohim) as he had done before (Dan 6:10). When he was thrown into the den, the lions didn't hurt him. Instead, those who had accused Daniel were thrown in along with their children and wives, and even before they reached the floor of the den the lions overpowered them and broke their bones in pieces (Dan 6:24). Their plans for evil came upon their own heads, just as in the case of Haman in the story of Esther.

Chapters 7 and 8 record dreams and visions of Daniel and their interpretations during the reign of Belshazzar, so these chapters belong chronologically between chapter 4 and chapter 5. In the first vision (ch. 7) Daniel saw four great beasts come out of the sea. They represented the same world governments as in Nebuchadnezzar's dream of an image: Babylon, Medo-Persia, Greece and Rome. But Daniel's dream went further by giving some details about the endtime antichrist government.

In the second vision (ch. 8) Daniel saw a ram with two horns (Media and Persia) and a male goat with a horn between the eyes (Alexander the

Great). The horn between the eyes broke and was replaced by four horns (Alexander's empire divided among four generals after his death). The vision continues to include Rome and the last-day antichrist government.

In the first year of Darius' reign, Daniel observed from Jeremiah's prophesy that the exile would last 70 years, after which they could return to Jerusalem, and that 70 years was now finished (Dan 9:2). So Daniel prayed that it might happen, which included confessing their sin and that Yahuah did right in sending them into exile (Dan 9:19). At the close of his prayer, the man Gabriel (a heavenly messenger) gave Daniel understanding regarding the end days. The information he gave is referred to as "the seventy weeks of Daniel" (Dan 9:24). Then follows a breakdown of the 70 weeks. The last week of those 70 weeks applies to us today:

> *And he will confirm the covenant with the many for one week* (seven years), *but in the middle of the week* (after 3½ years) *he will stop slaughter offerings and grain offerings* (Dan 9:27)..

This is a key verse having to do with the ministry of the last-day male son (man child, KJV).

> *And she* (the harlot church) *gave birth to **a son, a male** who is to shepherd all the nations with a rod of iron* (during the Millennium); *and her **child** was caught up* (raptured) *to Elohim and to his throne* (Rev 12:5).

Elohim made a covenant with Abraham, that his seed would be as numerous as the stars of the sky and as the sand of the seashore. This would include both Israel and gentiles. This verse (Dan 9:27) says that Elohim will confirm that covenant for one week, meaning seven years. Messiah confirmed the covenant to Israel with signs and wonders during his ministry of 3½ years. His death for our sins stopped the sacrifices, for he was the fulfillment of all the OT sacrifices. The Jews continued doing sacrifices until Rome destroyed Jerusalem in 70 A.D., but Yahuah didn't count them as sacrifices. There remains another 3½ years. That will be done by the male son/last-day bride of Messiah, again with signs and wonders to confirm the covenant to the gentiles. That 3½ years is rapidly approaching. We won't know when it starts, but we know when it ends. It ends with the rapture.

TWELVE MINOR PROPHETS

THE LAST TWELVE BOOKS of the Old Covenant scriptures are called the Minor Prophets. They are called minor because their books are short. In the Hebrew scriptures they are combined into one book. These books are not in the order in which they were written.

1. Hosea

HOSEA (ho-SHAY-ah) means salvation, just as does the last part of Yahushua's name. He prophesied during the reign of King Jeroboam II of Israel (the northern kingdom) while four successive kings—Uzziah, Jotham, Ahaz, and Hezekiah—were ruling in Judah. This means his prophetic ministry covered a period of about 40 years, from about 755 B.C. to about 715 B.C. His book was written some time during these years.

The book emphasizes Elohim's steadfast love for his covenant people, despite their continuing sin and rebellion. The prophet Hosea himself was an example of this steadfast love, for he was called to marry a prostitute. Yahuah told Hosea:

"Go, take for you a wife of prostitution, and children of prostitution, for the land has committed great prostitution by departing from Yahuah" (Hos 1:2).

This was to demonstrate to his people that they had been unfaithful to him because of serving false elohim.

Hosea obeyed, taking Gomer as wife, a prostitute. Soon after marriage she bore three children. According to the direction of Elohim, Hosea named them Jezreel (Elohim scatters), Lo-Ruhamah (not pitied), and Lo-Ammi (not my people). This was to show that Elohim was about to bring judgment on Israel because the people were serving false elohim. Just as the nation had rejected Elohim, Gomer eventually left Hosea and the children to return to her life of prostitution.

But Hosea continued loving his wife. He searched for her, found her at the slave market, bought her back, and restored her as his wife. What Hosea did was a prophetic act to show clearly that Elohim had not given up on Israel, although the people had "played the harlot" many times by returning to paganism and being enslaved to sin.

This is in the first three chapters of the book. Chapters 4-14 contain messages of judgment against Israel and Judah. The book ends by reminding the nation of Elohim's steadfast love. Despite their unfaithfulness, Elohim is determined to redeem them and restore them to their favored place as his covenant people.

Here are some notable passages.

> *"And I shall remove the names of the Baals*
> *From her mouth,* (that is, Babylonian words)
> *And they shall no more be remembered by their name.* (Hos 2:17).*

This will happen in the Millennium when Yahuah's people are fully converted.

> *"My people are destroyed for lack of the knowledge.*
> *Because you have rejected the knowledge,*
> *I reject you (as a nation) from being priest for me.*
> *Since you have forgotten the law of your Elohim,*
> *I also forget your children.*
> *"As they were increased* (in numbers, wealth, and power),
> *So they sinned against me.*
> *I will change their esteem into shame"* (Hos 4:6-7).

This is what happens when we sin, and this is what has happened to the assembly. We perish because we reject the knowledge of Elohim, and the esteem the assembly once had is now shame.

> *Come, and let us return to Yahuah.*
> *For he has torn but he heals us,*
> *He has stricken but he binds us up.*
> *After two days he shall revive us;*
> *On the third day he shall raise us up*
> *And we shall live before him* (Hos 6:1-2).

With Yahuah a day is as a thousand years (2Pe 3:8). The two days refer to the gentile assembly age, and the third day refers to the Millennium in which Israel rules with Yahushua Messiah as king.

> *So let us know, let us pursue to know Yahuah.*

His going forth is as certain as the morning.
And he shall come to us as the rain,
As the latter rain watering the earth (Hos 6:3).

The "latter rain" refers to the last-day outpouring of Yahuah's spirit upon the bride-company believers to bring in souls for the kingdom before the rapture.

For they have sown the wind
And shall reap the whirlwind (Hos 8:7).

The consequences of sin are great.

Sow for yourselves in righteousness,
Reap in kindness.
Break up your tillable ground (remove your wicked practices).
It is time to seek Yahuah,
Till he (the Father in the Son) *comes*
And rains righteousness on you (Hos 10:12).

"But I am Yahuah your Elohim from the land of Egypt,
And an elohim besides me you shall not know,
And there is no savior besides me" (Hos 13:4).
(Compare Is 45:21.)

2. Joel

JOEL (yoe-AIL) means Yahuah is Elohim. Hosea, the previous book, was a prophetic message to Israel (the northern kingdom) during its last days before Assyria conquered them and took them into exile. The book of Joel was to Judah (the southern kingdom), likely during its last days before Babylon conquered them and took them into exile. It is noted for prophesying about the outpouring of the spirit of Elohim on all people—a prophecy fulfilled several centuries later on the Day of Pentecost (compare Joel 2:28-32 with Act 2:14-21).

In chapters 1:1—2:11, the first section of this book, Joel introduces himself and speaks to his readers about their need to turn from their sins. In chapters 2:12—3:21, the second section of this book, the speaker is the all-powerful Elohim. He warns his people about the approaching day of judgment, and assures them of his continuing presence in spite of their unworthiness.

In the first section Joel calls attention to a devastating swarm of locusts that had recently swept through the land (Joel 1:4). These destructive locusts stripped the foliage from all trees, shrubs, and crops (Joel 1:7). The locust swarm and its devastation refers to the coming invasion of Babylon with their destruction. The people and livestock of Judah were facing the threat of starvation because of the famine that followed this invasion (Joel 1:15-18). As bad as this natural event had been, the prophet declares it will be as nothing in comparison to the coming day of Yahuah. This is the day of judgment when Elohim will pour his wrath upon his sinful and disobedient people. Joel also informs the people that this terrible day can be avoided. The way of escape is to turn to Elohim *"with all your heart, with fasting, and with mourning"* (Joel 2:12).

After Joel delivers his pleas for repentance, Elohim tells his wayward people that in spite of the famine, in the future there will be plenty to eat (2:18-19). This day of renewal will be marked by the outpouring of his spirit on all people (2:28-29). All the nations of the world will take notice as Elohim gathers his people together in the set-apart city of Jerusalem and they serve as their ruler:

> *"Judah shall abide forever,*
> > *And Jerusalem from generation to generation"* (Joel 3:20).

In Hosea we saw the truth of Elohim's steadfast mercy through the marriage of Hosea with a prostitute. In this book of Joel we see the truth of Elohim's judgment of sin through the invasion of locusts. Yes, Yahuah uses natural disasters to stir in his people a renewed awareness of his will. Any traumatic event of nature—flood, fire, storm, or earthquake—should motivate people to listen to the words of Yahuah, repent of their sins, and become fruitful for the kingdom.

> *Blow a shophar* (ram's horn) *in Zion*
> > *And sound an alarm in my set-apart mountain!*
> > *Let all the inhabitants of the earth tremble,*
> > *For the day of Yahuah is coming, for it is near* (Joel 2:1).

> *The day of Yahuah is great and very awesome,*
> > *And who can bear it?*
> > *"Yet even now," declares Yahuah,*
> > *"Turn to me with all your heart,*

And with fasting and with weeping and with mourning"
(Joel 2:11-12).

The Day of Yahuah is a day of judgment on the wicked. The final fulfillment of this prophecy is the plagues mentioned in the book of Revelation that occur just before Yahushua Messiah returns.

"And after this it shall be
That I pour out my spirit on all flesh.
And your sons and your daughters shall prophesy,
Your old men dream dreams,
Your young men see visions" (Joel 2:28).

As seen earlier, this applies to the day of Pentecost (Acts 2:17), and also to the Millennium.

3. Amos

Amos (ah-MOES) means "burden bearer." He was a prophet to the northern kingdom of Israel, the people always in idol worship and indulgent living. The book is in three major sections: 1) judgment against six gentile nations (Damascus, Gaza, Tyre, Edom, Ammon, Moab), and Judah and Israel (Am 1:3-2:16); 2) sermons of judgment against Israel (Am 3-6); and 3) visions of Elohim's judgment (Am 7:1-9:10). The book concludes with a promise of Israel's restoration (Am 9:11-15).

Amos uses a literary device of "three transgressions and four," giving the reasons for judgment. These are against Ammon and Judah:

Thus says Yahuah,
"For three transgressions of the sons of Ammon
and for four
I will not revoke its punishment,
Because they ripped open the pregnant women of Gilead
In order to enlarge their borders" (Am 1:13).

Thus says Yahuah,
"For three transgressions of Judah and for four
I will not revoke its punishment,
Because they rejected the Torah of Yahuah
And have not kept his requirements;
Their lies also have led them astray,

Those after which their fathers walked" (Am 2:4).

He calls the people *"cows of Bashan"* because of their wickedness (Am 4:1).

"Therefore … prepare to meet your Elohim, Israel" (Am 4:12).

"Seek Yahuah that you may live" (Am 5:6).

"Seek good and not evil, that you may live" (Am 5:14).

For thus says Adonai (Master) *Yahuah,*
  "The city going out by a thousand
    Has a hundred left,
  And that going out by a hundred
    Has ten left to the house of Israel" (Am 5:3).

This shows that only a remnant of Israel will be left on the earth at the beginning of the Millennium. This is similar to what we saw in the book of Joel.

Regarding the relationship of prophets to Yahuah, he says:

Surely Adonai (Master) *Yahuah will do nothing*
Unless he reveals his secret to his servants the prophets (Am 3:7).

We saw an example of this earlier when Elohim revealed to Abraham that he would destroy Sodom and Gomorrah because of their wickedness. This is still true today. The "prophets" of the prophetic movement today are mostly false, but there are some true ones.

Woe, you who wish for the day of Yahuah!
  For what purpose is the day of Yahuah for you?
  It will be darkness and not light (Am 5:18).

"The day of Yahuah" (day of the LORD) refers to his time of judgment. This particularly applies to the tribulation in the end times, but it also applies to any national disaster, whether by war or "nature."

Amos was a prophet calling for the righteousness and justice of Elohim, which is opposite of what liberals and the "politically correct" call it. He said:

Let justice roll down like water,
  And righteousness like a mighty stream (Am 5:24).

That's what we need to pray for.

Israel (in type, the assembly today) is measured by the righteousness of Yahuah, and no more is there forgiveness for their sin—it has reached to the full.

> *"Behold, I am setting a plumb-line*
> *In the midst of my people Israel,*
> *No longer do I pardon them"* (Am 7:8).

Amos described the nation of Israel as a basket of summer fruit, implying that it would soon spoil and rot in the blistering sun of Elohim's judgment (Am 8:1-3). Nevertheless:

> *"The days are coming," declares Yahuah,*
> *That the plowman will overtake the reaper,*
> *And the one who treads grapes him who sows seed"* (Am 9:13).

In type, this shows the quick harvest of souls in the last-day male-son/bride ministry.

Amos concludes with a promise to Israel that they will inherit the Promised Land: this promise to be fulfilled in the Millennium (Am 9:14-15).

4. Obadiah

OBADIAH IN HEBREW has two spellings, Ovadyah and Ovadyahu (oh-vahd-YAH and oh-vad-YAH-hoo). It is a combination of two words, *ovad* (servant) and Yahuah, so it means servant of Yahuah. Several men in the OT have this name. This prophet likely was a contemporary with Jeremiah and Ezekiel, which would be during the siege and final fall of Jerusalem by Babylon. The book is the shortest in the Old Testament, containing one chapter of only 21 verses.

The prophecy is against Edom, descendants of Esau, Jacob's twin brother, because of what they did. They mocked Israel and even participated in destroying and looting Jerusalem when it fell. Because of this great sin, Edom will be destroyed.

> *"For your violence against your brother Jacob,*
> *Shame shall cover you and you shall be cut off forever"* (Ob 1:10).

"For the day of Yahuah is near upon all the nations.
  As you [Edom] *have done, it shall be done to you;*
  Your reward shall return on your own head" (Ob 1:15).

We saw this principle at work in the book of Esther regarding Haman, and in the book of Daniel regarding those who had Daniel thrown into the lion's den. Thus it will be in the last-day plagues upon the nations just before Messiah returns. And Israel will be blessed by Elohim and restored to their native land (Ob 1:17).

5. Jonah

JONAH (yoe-NAW) is the same Jonah who prophesied during the reign of Jeroboam II of Israel, from 793 to 753 B.C. (2Ki 14:25). His book begins with Elohim's call to him to pronounce judgment against the great city of Nineveh, capital of the Assyrian empire. Besides serving false elohim, Assyria was an enemy of Israel and, because of Israel's sin, Assyria would eventually destroy Israel. Assyria was noted for being very cruel against those whom they conquered.

  But Jonah rose up to flee ... from the presence of Yahuah ... and **went down** *to Joppa, ...* **went down** *into* [the ship], *... had* **gone down** *into the lowest parts of the ship...*(Jon 1:3,5)..

When a person runs away from Elohim's call, he keeps going down spiritually.

"When my soul fainted within me,
  I remembered Yahuah.
  And my prayer went up to you,
  Into your set-apart temple" (Jon 2:7).

Yahuah knows how to bring us into a place where we will repent and obey.

  And Jonah ... cried out and said, "Yet forty days, and Nineveh shall be overthrown!" (Jon 3:4).

Jonah's message was about judgment, not repentance. Yet the people repented anyway, and Elohim heard and held back the judgment. That judgment, however, would come later.

  And he prayed to Yahuah, and he said, "Please, Yahuah, was this not what I said while I was in my own land? Therefore I fled to Tarshish. For I know that you are an Ĕl (AIL, shortened form of Elohim) *showing favor, and compassionate, patient and of great kindness, and relenting from doing evil"* (Jon 4:2).

We see here the reason Jonah fled from the call. Even though his message was judgment with no mention of repentance, he knew that if the city repented, that Yahuah would hold back the judgment. And Jonah wanted them destroyed. Why? Because he knew that if Nineveh were not destroyed, Assyria would destroy Israel, the northern kingdom. But Elohim wanted Assyria to be around so he (Elohim) could use them as the instrument of judgment against Israel. Then he would use Babylon to destroy Assyria.

But Jonah, instead of obeying Elohim's command and heading to Nineveh, caught a ship traveling in the opposite direction. Elohim, however, knows how to get his people to obey him. His method for Jonah was to bring a great storm so that the sailors despaired of life. When they learned that the reason for the storm was because Jonah had disobeyed Elohim, at Jonah's request they threw him into the sea. The storm stopped, and Jonah was swallowed by a great fish.

After three days and three nights inside the fish, Jonah repented, and the fish vomited him out on shore. Yahushua spoke of this event saying he would be in the grave for three days and three nights (Mt 12:40). This time Jonah obeyed Elohim's command and went to Nineveh to proclaim the judgment. Very likely the people there had heard of what happened to Jonah and so were open to believe his message.

Jonah didn't like it that Nineveh repented and escaped Elohim's punishment, so he was angry. To teach the prophet a lesson, as Jonah was sitting on a hill overlooking the city to see what would happen, Elohim raised up a gourd vine to shade him from the sun, then caused a worm to cut it down and brought a hot wind from the east to add to Jonah's misery. When Jonah complained about the missing plant, Elohim reminded him that he was an Elohim of compassion who had the right to love and forgive the pagan Assyrians or any other people who turned to him in obedience and faith. Jonah had been angry about a plant, while Elohim wants to save people.

143

6. Micah

THE NAME MICAH (mee-KAH) is a combination of three words, *mi* (meaning who), *ki* (meaning like), and *ah* (shortened form of Yahuah). So it means, "Who is like Yahuah?" He was a companion prophet with Isaiah and prophesied against both Israel (the northern kingdom), and Judah (the southern kingdom). Both nations were in serious immorality and idolatry. Elohim used Assyria for judging them both. This was some years after Jonah's prophecy. Assyria conquered Israel, but failed to conquer Judah. Then Elohim used Babylon to conquer Assyria and then Judah.

Here are some key verses.

Woe to those who scheme iniquity,
  Who work out evil on their beds!
  When morning comes they do it,
  For it is in the power of their hands.
They covet fields and then seize them,
  And houses and take them away.
  They oppress (rob) a man and his house,
  A man and his inheritance (Mi 2:1-2).

This is an example of why their wickedness will bring destruction on themselves, and why Yahuah won't answer them when they cry to him for help (Mi 3:4). Nevertheless, after judgment they will have peace. But this will be in the Millennium when all nations will be at peace and submitted to Yahuah in Jerusalem, the capital of Israel and of the world.

And in the latter days (the Millennium) *it shall be*
  That the mountain (nation) of the house of Yahuah
    Is established on the top of the mountains (the nations),
    And shall be exalted above the hills (lesser nations).
    And peoples shall flow to it.
And many nations shall come and say,
  "Come, and let us go up to the mountain of Yahuah,
    To the House of the Elohim of Jacob,
    And let him teach us his ways
    And let us walk in his paths."

For out of Zion comes forth the Torah
  And the word of Yahuah from Jerusalem."
And he shall judge among many peoples
  And reprove strong nations afar off.
  They shall beat their swords into plowshares
    And their spears into pruning hooks—
  Nation shall not lift up sword against nation
    Neither teach battle any more (Mi 4:1-3)..

In this book we have the announcement of Messiah's birth place.

"But you, Bethlehem Ephrathah,
  You who are little among the clans of Judah,
  Out of you shall come forth to me
  The one to become ruler in Israel.
  And his comings forth are of old,
    From everlasting" (Mi 5:2). (See Mt 2:6.)

We also see the definition of true religion, another way of saying the two greatest commandments.

He has declared to you, man, what is good.
  And what does Yahuah require of you,
  But to do right and to love kindness
  And to walk humbly with your Elohim? (Mi 6:8).

And we also see that Elohim gets rid of the sins of believers:

Who is an Ĕl (ail) *like you, who pardons sin*
  And passes over the transgression
  Of the remnant of his inheritance?
He shall not retain his anger forever,
  For he delights in kindness.
  He shall turn back;
He shall have compassion on us;
  He shall trample upon our wickedness
  And throw all our sins into the depths of the sea! (Mi 7:18-19).

This is what Yahuah does for us when we give our lives to his Son Yahushua Messiah.

7. Nahum

NAHUM (nah-KHOOM) means "comfortable." This book foretells the destruction of the nation of Assyria and its capital city, Nineveh. Nineveh fell about 612 B.C. Therefore, the book was probably written shortly before this time. The book of Revelation speaks of seven world governments. The first was Egypt. Elohim used Assyria to conquer Egypt, making it the second world government, then used Assyria, in 722 B.C., to conquer wicked Israel (the northern kingdom), then used Babylon to conquer Assyria. As noted above, Nineveh, the capital of Assyria, fell to Babylon about 612 B.C. The entire Assyrian Empire crumbled three years later under Babylon. Yahuah uses nations, even wicked ones, to judge nations.

Yahuah is a jealous and revenging Ĕl.
Yahuah is one who takes revenge
And is a possessor of wrath.
Yahuah takes vengeance on his adversaries
And he watches for his enemies.
Yahuah is slow to anger and great in power,
But by no means leaves unpunished.
Yahuah has his way in the whirlwind and in the storm,
And the clouds are the dust of his feet (Na 1:2-3).

These introductory verses in Nahum declare:

"Vengeance is mine, I shall repay," says Yahuah (Rom 12:19; see also Dt 32:35). (Not quoted in Nahum, but the idea is there.)

Yahuah is good, a stronghold in the day of trouble.
And he knows those who take refuge in him.
But with an overwhelming flood
He makes a complete end of (Nineveh's) *place,*
And darkness will pursue his enemies (Na 1:7-8).

Jonah's desire that Nineveh be destroyed is now being fulfilled, but it was after Assyria had finished its purpose in Elohim's plan.

See, on the mountains the feet of him who brings good news,
Who proclaims peace! (Na 1:15).(See Isa 52:7; Ro 10:15).

The "good news" in this context is that Nineveh is destroyed. In type, the good news is that the power of Satan in our lives is destroyed when we give our lives to Yahushua.

8. Habakkuk

HABAKKUK (khah-vah-KOOK) means "embrace." This book deals with the problems of evil and human suffering. It speaks of the coming destruction of Judah, so it was written some time before Jerusalem was destroyed by the Babylonians in 587 B.C., perhaps about 600 B.C.

Habakkuk complains to Yahuah about the success of the wicked as though Elohim doesn't care. But in the end the wicked will be destroyed. At the time when he received this vision, Babylon had already defeated Assyria and Egypt. The implication is that Habakkuk's nation, Judah, will be the next to fall. Elohim assures him that Babylon will prevail, not because they are righteous, but because they are temporary instruments of judgment in his hands (Hab 2:4).

> *"But the righteous one lives by his faithfulness"* (Hab 2:4b).
> (Quoted in Ro 1:17; Gal 3:11; Heb 10:38).

Then he pronounces five burdens of woe against the nation of Babylon (Hab 2:6,9,12,15,19). Elohim will not be mocked; the end of Babylon is as certain as the judgment they will bring on Judah. In all of this Elohim will vindicate his righteous character:

> *For the earth will be filled*
> *With the knowledge of the esteem of Yahuah*
> *As the waters cover the sea* (Hab 2:14).. (See Is 11:9.)

This will happen in the Millennium.

After this assurance, in chapter 3, we have a beautiful psalm of praise to Yahuah.

> *Though the fig tree does not blossom*
> *Nor is there fruit in the vines*
> *And the harvest of the olive has failed*
> *And the fields yield no food*
> *And the flock has been cut off from the fold*
> *And there is no herd in the stalls,*
> *Yet I rejoice in Yahuah,*
> *I joy in the Elohim of my salvation.*

Yahuah Adonai (Master) *is my strength*
And he makes my feet like those of a deer
And makes me walk on my high places (Hab 3:17-19).

Despite trials and no matter how bad things appear, we have a reason for praise.

"Rejoice in Yahuah always" (Php 4:4).

9. Zephaniah

ZEPHANIAH IN HEBREW has two spellings, Tsefanyah and Tsefan-yahu (tseh-fawn-YAH and Tseh-fawn-YAH-hoo). It means "Yahuah has hidden." This man prophesied in Judah (the southern kingdom) during the reign of good king Josiah. Josiah tried to rid the nation of its idolatry, but the people remained wicked, and so Yahuah proclaimed judgment against the nation and Jerusalem. He also proclaimed judgment against the surrounding nations. Eventually, however, Elohim will restore Judah. This will be during the Millennium.

"And I will stretch out my hand against Judah
And against all the inhabitants of Jerusalem
And cut off every trace of Baal from this place,
The names of the idolatrous priests with the priests
And those on the house-tops bowing down to the host
of the heavens ,
And those bowing themselves swearing by Yahuah
And swearing by Malkam (national idol of the Ammonites)
And those who turn away from following Yahuah
And who have not sought Yahuah or inquired of him" (Zeph
1:4-6).

This passage applies to the assembly today, for the assembly today is full of Babylon.

Near is the great day of Yahuah,
Near and hurrying greatly, the noise of the day of Yahuah.
Let the mighty man then bitterly cry out!
That day is a day of wrath,
A day of distress and trouble,
A day of waste and ruin,

A day of darkness and gloom,
A day of clouds and thick darkness,
A day of shophar (ram's horn) *and alarm,*
Against the walled cities
And against the high towers.
"And I shall bring distress on mankind,
And they shall walk like blind men,
Because they have sinned against Yahuah,
And their blood shall be poured out like dust
And their flesh like dung" (Zeph 1:14-17).

The immediate fulfillment of this prophecy was the fall of Jerusalem. But it goes beyond that to the plagues on the nations mentioned in the book of Revelation.

Seek Yahuah,
All you meek of the earth,
Who have done his judgment.
Seek righteousness, seek meekness,
If perhaps you will be hidden
In the day of wrath of Yahuah (Zeph 2:3).

This applies to the rapture of the bride company of believers before the great tribulation.

"Therefore wait upon me," declares Yahuah,
"Until the day I rise up for plunder
        (the last-day plagues).
For my judgment is to gather nations,
To assemble kingdoms (Armageddon)
To pour out on them all my fierce displeasure,
My burning wrath.
For by the fire of my jealousy
All the earth shall be devoured.
"For then I shall turn to the peoples a pure language,
That they all call on the name of Yahuah,
To serve him with one shoulder" (Zeph 3:8-9).
        (all working together in unity)

After the plagues to destroy wickedness, then there will be purity in the Millennium.

"At that time I shall bring you in,
Even at the time I gather you,
For I shall give you for a name and for a praise
Among all the peoples of the earth,
When I turn back your captivity before your eyes,"
said Yahuah (Zeph 3:20).

10. Haggai

HAGGAI (khahg-GAH-ee) means "festive." The purpose of this book is to encourage the people of Israel who had returned to their native land of Judah after the captivity in Babylon. In particular, it is to rebuild the temple, to remain faithful to Elohim's promises, to be set-apart and enjoy Elohim's provisions, and to keep their hope set on the return of the coming Messiah and the establishment of his kingdom. He delivered these messages of encouragement *"in the second year of King Darius"* (Hag 1:1), a Persian ruler. This dates his book in 520 BCE.

For more than 50 years Israel was in captivity in Babylon, and then in Persia after Persia conquered Babylon. When they were allowed to return to their land, a remnant returned; and at first they were diligent in rebuilding the temple. But they grew tired of the project and stopped and spent time rebuilding their own houses. Haggai's message was to motivate them to resume the project. This is a type of sinners who, upon being saved, are at first zealous for Messiah, but then become lukewarm.

Thus says Yahuah of armies, saying, "This people have said, 'The time has not come, the time that the house (temple) *of Yahuah is to be built.'"*

Then the word of Yahuah came by Haggai the prophet, saying, "Is it time for you yourselves to dwell in your paneled houses, and this house (the temple) *be in ruins?"*

And now, thus said Yahuah of armies, "Consider your ways! You have sown much, but brought in little; you eat, but do not have enough; you drink, but you are not filled with drink; you clothe yourselves but no one is warm; and he who earns wages earns wages to put into a bag with holes" (Hag 1:2-6).

The bad things that happen in our lives teach us to consider our ways and to find out if our focus on the things of this life is hindering our relationship with Yahuah.

> *For thus said Yahuah of armies, "Once more, in a little while, and I am shaking the heavens and earth, the sea and dry land. And I shall shake all the nations, and they shall come to the Delight of all the nations, and I shall fill this house with esteem," said Yahuah of armies. "The silver is mine and the gold is mine," declares Yahuah of armies. The esteem of this latter house shall be greater than the former," said Yahuah of armies. "And in this place I give peace," declares Yahuah of armies* (Hag 2:6-9).

The shaking of nations refers to the endtime plagues before Messiah's return. The Delight of all the nations is Yahushua Messiah, and the remnant that survives the plagues to enter the Millennial kingdom will find him as their delight. The following passage says the same thing in different words. The governor Zerubbabel is a type of Messiah.

> *"And I shall overturn the throne of kingdoms. And I shall destroy the might of the gentile kingdoms and overturn the chariots and their riders. And the horses and their riders shall come down, each by the sword of his brother."*
>
> *Yahuah of armies declares, "In that day I shall take you, Zerubbabel my servant, ... and shall make you as a signet, for I have chosen you," declares Yahuah of armies* (Hag 2:22-23).

11. Zechariah

ZECHARIAH IN HEBREW has two spellings, Z^ekaryah and Z^ekaryahu (zeh-kar-YAH and zeh-kar-YAH-hoo). It means "Yahuah is remembered" or "Yahuah remembered."

From Easton's Bible Dictionary:

> A prophet of Judah. ... His prophetical career began in the second year of Darius (520 B.C.), about sixteen years after the return of the first company from exile. He was contemporary with Haggai (Ezra 5:1).
>
> His book consists of two distinct parts, (1) chapters 1 to 8, inclusive, and (2) 9 to the end. It begins with a preface (1:1-6), which recalls the nation's past history, for the purpose of

presenting a solemn warning to the present generation. Then follows a series of eight visions (1:7-6:8), succeeding one another in one night, which may be regarded as a symbolical history of Israel, intended to furnish consolation to the returned exiles and stir up hope in their minds. The symbolical action, the crowning of Joshua (6:9-15), describes how the kingdoms of the world become the kingdom of God's Christ.

Chapters 7 and 8, delivered two years later, are an answer to the question whether the days of mourning for the destruction of the city should be any longer kept, and an encouraging address to the people, assuring them of God's presence and blessing.

The second part of the book (ch. 9-14) bears no date. It is probable that a considerable interval separates it from the first part. It consists of two burdens.

The first burden (ch. 9-11) gives an outline of the course of God's providential dealings with his people down to the time of the Advent [the coming of Messiah].

The second burden (ch. 12-14) points out the glories that await Israel in "the latter day", the final conflict and triumph of God's kingdom.

(Easton's Bible Dictionary)

The book of Zechariah has too many difficult things in it for this survey to comment on. Many have to do with endtime events and are parallel with visions in the book of Revelation. Here are a few verses with comments.

And he showed me Joshua (Heb Yahushua) *the high priest standing before a messenger of Yahuah and Satan standing at his right hand to accuse him. And Yahuah said to Satan, "Yahuah rebuke you, Satan! Yahuah who has chosen Jerusalem rebuke you! Is this* (remnant that came back from captivity) *not a brand plucked from the fire* (of chastisement)*?"* (Zec 3:1-2).

This is interesting regarding Satan. In the book of Job, Satan stood before Yahuah to be an adversary of Job.

"Not by might nor by power but by my spirit," said Yahuah of armies (Zec 4:6).

Many sermons have been given on this verse. Even Yahushua did not operate by his own power, but by Yahuah's spirit.

The following is a prophesy of the Millennium. It does not refer to Israel becoming a nation in 1948 or to Jews today from around the world returning to Israel, for Israel is still in rebellion against Elohim. They will not be his people until they repent at the time Yahushua returns to establish his 1,000-year rule.

> *Thus said Yahuah of armies, "Behold, I shall save my people from the land of the sunrise* (the east) *and from the land of the sunset* (the west). *And I shall bring them back and they shall dwell in the midst of Jerusalem. And they shall be my people and I shall be their Elohim in truth and in righteousness"* (Zec 8:7-8).

The following is a prophecy of the coming Messiah.

> *Rejoice greatly, daughter of Zion!*
>   *Shout, daughter of Jerusalem!*
>   *Behold, your king is coming to you.*
>   *He is righteous and having deliverance,*
>   *Humble and riding on a donkey,*
>   *A colt, a foal of a donkey* (Zec 9:9)..

The following is a prophecy regarding the battle of Armageddon.

> *"Behold, I* (Yahuah) *make Jerusalem a cup of reeling to all the people around and also against Judah. It is in the siege against Jerusalem. And in that day I shall make Jerusalem a very heavy stone for all the peoples—all who try to lift it will hurt themselves. And all the nations of the earth shall be gathered against it* (Zec 12:2-3)..

The next selection is a prophecy regarding the second coming of Yahushua. The context is the coming of Yahuah, but he comes in his Son. When the Jews see him come, a remnant of them will repent and finally recognize that Yahushua is their Messiah.

> *"And I shall pour on the house of David and on the inhabitants of Jerusalem a spirit of favor and prayers. And they shall look on me whom they pierced, and they shall mourn for him as one mourns for his only* (son). *And they shall be in bitterness over him as a bitterness over the first-born"* (Zec 12:10).

In chapter 14, when Yahushua returns, the Mount of Olives splits in two and living waters flow from Jerusalem toward the Mediterranean and toward the Dead Sea.

12. Malachi

MALACHI (mal-ah-KEE) means "my messenger." He wrote his prophecy about 450 B.C., which was about 100 years after Judah returned from captivity in Babylon. Portions of his prophecy are written in the format of a debate; that is, Elohim makes a statement of truth, the people deny it, and he refutes their denial, restating and proving the truth of his original statement (Mal 1:2-7; 2:10-17; 3:7-10).

From Easton's Bible Dictionary:

MALACHI, BOOK OF
The contents of the book ... consist of three sections, preceded by an introduction (Mal 1:1-5), in which the prophet reminds Israel of Jehovah's love to them. The first section (1:6-2:9) contains a stern rebuke addressed to the priests who had despised the name of Jehovah, and been leaders in a departure from his worship and from the covenant, and for their partiality in administering the law. In the second (2:9-16) the people are rebuked for their intermarriages with idolatrous heathen. In the third (2:17-4:6) he addresses the people as a whole, and warns them of the coming of the God of judgment, preceded by the advent of the Messiah.

This book is frequently referred to in the New Testament (Matt 11:10; 17:12; Mark 1:2; 9:11,12; Luke 1:17; Rom 9:13).

(Easton's Bible Dictionary)

"For from the rising of the sun even to its going down my name is great among nations (i.e. the gentiles). *And in every place incense is offered to my name and a clean offering. For my name is great among nations," said Yahuah of armies* (Mi 1:11).

"Behold, I am sending my messenger (Heb *malachi*) *and he shall prepare a way before me. Then suddenly the Master* (Heb *adon*) *you are seeking comes to his temple, even the messenger of the covenant in whom you delight. See, he is coming," said Yahuah of armies.*

And who is able to bear the day of his coming, and who is able to stand when he appears? For he is like a refiner's fire and like a launderer's soap.

And he shall sit as a refiner and a cleanser of silver, and he shall cleanse the sons of Levi (i.e. the priests and a type of believers in

Messiah) *and refine them as gold and silver, and they shall belong to Yahuah, bringing near an offering in righteousness* (Mi 3:1-3).

This passage shows that the result of the second coming is a people who have become righteous.

"Would a man rob Elohim? Yet you are robbing me! But you said, 'In what have we robbed you?' In the tithe and the offering! (Mi 3:8).

They were bringing tithes and offerings, but what they were bringing was unacceptable, thus showing their hard heart.

"Behold, I am sending you Elijah the prophet before the coming of the great and awesome day of Yahuah. And he shall turn the heart of the fathers to the children and the heart of the children to their fathers, lest I come and smite the earth with utter destruction" (Mi 4:5-6).

These are the last verses of Malachi and of the OT scriptures. Elijah would not come in person, but as a ministry. John the Immerser (John the Baptist) had this ministry as did Yahushua, and as will the bride company of believers in the last days. This is what we are doing when we share the good news of what Yahushua has done to bring us salvation, so that they may be reconciled to our Father.

THE INTER-TESTAMENT PERIOD

(The following is adapted from bibleinst.com, author unknown, not copyrighted.)

THIS PERIOD GIVES A BACKGROUND to the understanding of the New Testament.

THE PERIOD IN GENERAL

With the Old Testament canon closing with Malachi around 397 B.C., we see that this period between Malachi and Matthew covers some four hundred years. This four hundred year interval has been called "the dark period" of Israel's history in pre-Christian times, because during it there was neither prophet nor inspired writer. With this period we seem to find the fulfillment of Psalm 74:9 upon Israel:

"We see not our signs;
There is no more any prophet;

Neither is there among us any that knows how long" (Ps 74:9).

The condition of the Jews as a nation and race at the beginning of this four hundred year period should be kept in mind. Two hundred years earlier Jerusalem had been overthrown and the Jewish people carried into the Babylonian exile (606 B.C. - 586 B.C.) as punishment for their unfaithfulness to Yahuah. At the end of this 70-years' punishment period, the Babylonian empire having been overthrown and succeeded by that of Media-Persia (536 B.C.), Cyrus, the Persian emperor issued a decree permitting the return of the Jews to Israel.

Under the leadership of Zerubbabel some 50,000 Jews returned. Some twenty years after their return, after many setbacks, the building of the Temple was completed in 516 B.C. Then after another 58 years had passed, in 458 B.C. Ezra the scribe returned to Jerusalem with a small group of Israel and restored the Torah (Law) and the ritual. Still another 13 years later, in 445 B.C. Nehemiah had come to Jerusalem to rebuild the walls and become governor. Now, once again, there was a Jewish state in Judea, though under Persian rule.

This is the picture of the Jewish people at the beginning of the four hundred year period between Malachi and Matthew: the Jewish Remnant back in Judea for about one hundred and forty years (536 B.C. - 397 B.C.), a small, dependent Jewish state there, Jerusalem and the temple rebuilt, the Torah and the ritual restored, but with the mass of the people remaining dispersed throughout the Medo-Persian empire.

THE POLITICAL DEVELOPMENT

Viewed politically, the varying course of the Jewish nation in Palestine simply reflects the history of the different world empires which ruled Palestine. The one exception to this was the Maccabean revolt [revolt of Maccabeus] which resulted for a short period in which they became an independent Jewish government.

Jewish history during those four centuries between the Testaments runs in six periods: the Persian, the Greek, the Egyptian, the Syrian, the Maccabean and the Roman.

1. THE PERSIAN PERIOD (536 - 333 B.C.)

The Persian rule over Palestine, which commenced with the

decree of Cyrus in 536 B.C. for the return of the Jewish Remnant, continued until 333 B.C., when Palestine fell under the power of Alexander the Great (the third of the Gentile world-empires foretold by Daniel). This means that at the end of Malachi the Jews were still under Persian rule and remained so for about the first sixty years of the inter-testament period.

Persian rule seems to have been tolerant. The high priest form of Jewish government was respected with the high priest being given an increasing degree of civil power in addition to his religious offices, though, of course, he was responsible to the Persian governor of Syria.

2. THE GREEK PERIOD (333 - 323 B.C.)

Alexander the Great is a phenomenon in history. He came into leadership through the assassination of his father when he, Alexander, was but twenty years of age. He transformed the face of the world, politically, in little more than a decade. He is the "notable horn" in the "he-goat" vision of Daniel (Dan 8:1-7).

In his march on Jerusalem he not only spared the city, but also offered sacrifice to Yahuah and had the prophecies of Daniel read to him concerning the overthrow of the Persian empire by a king of Grecia (Dan 8:21.) Thereafter he treated the Jews with respect and gave them full rights of citizenship with the Greeks in his new city, Alexandria, and in other cities. This in return created decidedly pro-Greek sympathies among the Jews, and, along with Alexander's spreading of the Greek language and civilization, a Hellenistic (i.e. Grecian) spirit developed among the Jews which greatly affected their mental outlook afterward.

3. THE EGYPTIAN PERIOD (323 - 204 B.C.)

This is the longest of the six periods of the inter-testament period. The death of Alexander resulted in a period of confusion which was resolved by Alexander's empire being divided under four generals: Ptolemy, Lysimachus, Cassander and Selenus. These are the four "notable ones" which take the place of the "great horn," as prophesied in Daniel 8:21,22.

After severe fighting, Judea, along with the rest of Syria, fell to Ptolemy Soter, the first of the Greek kings to rule over Egypt. This was the beginning of the Ptolematic dynasty.

For a time Ptolemy Soter dealt harshly with the Jews, but afterwards became just as friendly. His successor, Ptolemy Philadelphus, continued this favorable attitude. His reign is notable in that the famous Septuagint translation of the Old Testament scriptures was made from the Hebrew into the Greek language. We see the importance of this when we realize that the Greek language had now become the language of the civilized world. The Jews were so numerous in Egypt and North Africa that such a translation had become necessary. The Septuagint came into general use well before the birth of Jesus, and was still in use during the time Jesus was on earth, and was quoted by Jesus.

4. THE SYRIAN PERIOD (204 - 165 B.C.)

There are two points of special note about this period. First, it was at this time that Palestine was divided into the five sections which we find in the New Testament. (Sometimes the first three of these collectively are called Judea.) These different provinces are: Judea, Samaria, Galilee, Perea, and Trachonitis.

Secondly, this Syrian period was the most tragic part of the intertestament era for the Jews of Judea. Antiochus the Great was harsh toward the Jews. So was his successor. Yet the Jews in Judea were still permitted to live under their own laws, administered by the high priest and his council. But with the accession of Antiochus Epiphanes (175-164 B.C.) a "reign of terror" fell upon the Jews. In 170 B.C. Jerusalem was plundered, the wall torn down, the temple desecrated, temple sacrifices were abolished, the Most Set-apart Place was stripped of its costly furniture, Jewish religion was banned, a pig was sacrificed on the altar, and the Temple at Jerusalem was rededicated to Jupiter Olympius with a statue of Jupiter Olympius erected on the altar, and the people were subjected to monstrous cruelties.

5. THE MACCABEAN PERIOD (165-63 B.C.)

This excessiveness by Antiochus provoked the Jews to revolt and resist. Judas Maccabeus (Judas means hammer) gathered around him a large army of fighters, and after several victories assumed the offensive. Jerusalem was captured, the temple refurnished, and on 25th December, the anniversary of its being polluted three years earlier, the orthodox sacrifices were reinstituted (which date the Jews still observed as the Feast of the Dedication: see John 10:22). Judas Maccabeus also captured the chief military posts up and down the land. Antiochus is said to have died in a state of raving madness.

During this period Judas Maccabeus was killed. In 143 B.C. Simon, the brother of Judas, assumed leadership of the army. He was able to capture all other Syrian strongholds in Judea and forced the Syrian garrison in the citadel at Jerusalem to surrender.

Thus Judea was freed of all alien troops, and from that time (about 142 B.C.) was once again under independent Jewish government. Except for one short lapse, this continued until Judea became a Roman province, in 63 B.C.

6. THE ROMAN PERIOD (63 B.C. onward)

The Herod family now appears on the scene. Antipater, the father of the Herod who reigned at the time of Messiah's birth, managed to secure the support of Roman general Pompey to gain control of Judea. The result was a siege of Jerusalem which lasted three months with Pompey taking the city. Pompey, with disregard for the Temple, strolled into the Most Set-apart Place, an action which at once estranged all loyal Jewish hearts toward the Romans. That was 63 B.C

Pompey's subjugation of Jerusalem ended the period of Judea's regained independence. Judea now became a province of the Roman empire. The high priest was completely deprived of any royal status and retained priestly function only. The governing power was exercised by Antipater, who was appointed procurator of Judea by Julius Cesar in 47 B.C.

Antipater appointed his son Herod as governor of Galilee when Herod was only fifteen years old. In about 40 B.C., after appealing to Rome, Herod was appointed king of the Jews. He greatly increased the splendor of Jerusalem, building the elaborate temple which was the center of Jewish worship in the time of Messiah.

However, he was as cruel and sinister as he was able and ambitious. He stained his hands with many murders. He slew all three of his wife's brothers—Antigonus, Aristobulus and Hyrcanus. Later he murdered even his wife. Again, later, he murdered his mother-in-law. And still later he murdered his own sons by Marianne. This is that "Herod the Great" who was king when Messiah was born.

Such, then, in brief, is the political history of the Jews in Palestine during the four-hundred-year period between Malachi and Matthew.

THE RELIGIOUS AND SPIRITUAL DEVELOPMENT

Not only had Palestine changed hands half a dozen times, there are new sects or parties: Pharisees, Sadducees and Herodians. There are new institutions: Synagogue, Scribes and Sanhedrin. These changes—the rise of these new sects and institutions, and the evolutions of Judaism—the evolving of the people and their religion around the Old Testament scriptures into one and the same, one implying the other—have come about during those four hundred years between the Old Testament and the New. This in itself shows the importance attached to the inter-testament period.

This system of Jewish religion, which originated just after the Exile and developed during the inter-testament period, was founded on a new zeal for the Law (the sacred scriptures) and the Messianic hope which came forth from those scriptures. This hope concerned the coming Messiah who would permanently gather together and exalt the chosen people, and under whose esteemed reign all the promised blessings of the covenant made with Abraham would be fulfilled.

SYNAGOGUE

The Law now became the standard of set-apartness and the symbol of nationality. Thus the rise of the local synagogue. For here the scriptures were read and expounded by the scribes.

The basic idea of the synagogue was instruction in the scriptures, not worship, even though an elaborate liturgical service developed later with public prayers read by appointed persons and responses made by the congregation. (See Mt 4:23, 9:35; Luke 4:15, 44; Acts 5:15, 14:1, 17:10, 18:19.)

However, from that time, also, there began to form an elaborate system of interpretations, amplifications and additional regulations, which resulted in the religion of Judaism at the time of Yahushua.

SCRIBES

The scribes of Old Testament times were different from that which developed during the inter-testament period and had acquired such important status in Messiah's time.

160

It is not difficult to see how, when once this new order of scribes came in, it rapidly gained great power. The very nature of this new Judaism was to make every Jew personally responsible for the keeping of the whole Law. Therefore, "a definite rule" had somehow to be extracted from the Law to cover practically every activity of daily life. To accomplish this there had to be a body of trained experts who made the study of the Law the great business of their lives.

Thus the scribes whom we meet in the Gospel narratives were a class of professional experts in the interpretation and application of the Law and the other Old Testament scriptures. In the Greek of the New Testament their usual title is the plural, *grammateis*, translated as "scribes." Less frequently they are called "lawyers," *nomikoi*, as in Luke 7:30.

It is with Ezra that the office of the scribe reaches a new dignity. In Nehemiah 8:1-8 we see Ezra elevated in a pulpit, reading and expounding and applying the Law, with Levite assistants, *"causing the people to understand the Law."*

PHARISEES

The Pharisees must be distinguished from the scribes, although in the Gospels they are often mentioned together (Matthew 5:20, 12:38, 15:1, 23:2, Mark 2:16, Luke 5:21,30, etc.). The Pharisees were a religious party held together by their peculiar aims and views, whereas the scribes were a body of experts in a scholastic sense. A man might be both a Pharisee and a scribe; in fact, practically all the scribes were Pharisees in outlook and association; yet the two parties were different from each other.

It was inevitable that the Pharisees should have much in common with the scribes, those specialists in the Written Law, and in the ever enlarging Oral Law. (The Oral Law was a complex code of application of the Written Law to every area of one's life and activities.) Most of those who were scribes by vocation would be Pharisees in conviction.

We see the spirit of Phariseeism in the aim of Ezra and leaders of the Jewish remnant as expressed in Nehemiah 10:28,29. It is a spirit of "separatism" from all others to Yahuah through a strict observance of his Law. By common consent all mixed marriages were dissolved and other irregularities corrected. In a mass meeting and by signed covenant the book of the Law was acclaimed as the binding standard for both state and individual. Separation to Yahuah was the controlling idea. Separatism based on the Law (Written and Oral) was the ideology of the Pharisees.

The thing, however, that eventually crystallized them into a sect was a body of Jews, primarily made up of the priests, whose goal and interest was the worldly aspects of religion and politics. Thus we have the Pharisees on one side and the Sadducees on the other.

The Pharisees as a body were influential way beyond their numbers. According to Josephus, the number of Pharisees in Herod's time was only about 6,000. Yet, despite their small number, they had in fact such a hold on the popular mind that no governing power could afford to disregard them. The mark of the Pharisee—the ritualist—is that he is always ADDING TO scripture.

SADDUCEES

The Sadducees were a much smaller body than the Pharisees, and belonged for the most part to the wealthy and influential priestly families who were the aristocrats of the Jewish nation. The leaders of the party were the elders with seats in the council, the military officers, and the statesmen and officials who took part in the management of public affairs. With the mass of the people they never had much influence; like true aristocrats, they did not greatly care for it.

As a body they rejected totally the Oral Law accumulated by the scribes and held to by the Pharisees, and professed to stand by the Written Law alone; though, even their stand on the Written Law alone was done so with great skepticism. They denied the bodily resurrection, and did not believe either in angels or spirits (Mt 22:23 and Acts 23:8).

HERODIANS

This is a political group, and the leading aim of its members was to further the cause of the Herod government. This group was hated by the Pharisees. The two parties were bitterly intolerant of each other, which makes the joining of the Pharisees with the Herodians against Yahushua all the more astonishing.

SANHEDRIN

The Sanhedrin was the supreme judicial and administrative

council of the Jewish people, made up of 71 people.

THE COMMON PEOPLE

The common people, far removed from the political and religious parties, were waiting for the consolation of Israel. And now at last, as we enter into the New Testament times, it was to such as these that the long expected Messiah had been revealed.

(end of adaption from bibleinst.com)

The Judaism at the time of Yahushua was a sterile religion of tradition and paganism, although among them there were righteous people. Yahushua was a prophet that came to expose their sin and call them to repentance, *"for the kingdom of Elohim is near."*

TWENTYSEVEN NEW COVENANT SCRIPTURES

ALMOST ALL OF THIS SURVEY is on the Old Covenant books. What follows are a few comments on each of the New Covenant books.

FIVE HISTORY BOOKS

1-4. The Life of Yahushua

THE FOUR GOSPELS give the life of Yahushua. The first three are called "synoptic gospels," because they are similar in viewpoint and material. Their main focus is Yahushua's ministry in Galilee. Matthew and Luke both have birth stories of Yahushua. Their stories differ in that Matthew has wise men coming with three gifts, and Luke has the birth in a stable and shepherds coming to do homage. In contrast, Mark begins with the ministry of John the Immerser (Baptist) to make the way for the coming of the Messiah.

Mark is a Gospel of action, portraying the **Messiah as servant** with very few parables. A parable is a story in everyday life illustrating a spiritual truth. Both Matthew and Luke have many parables, some the same and some different. **Matthew** portrays the **Messiah as king**, whereas **Luke** portrays **Messiah as man**.

The focus of **John's Gospel** is Yahushua's ministry in Judea. It portrays **Yahushua as the Son of Elohim** and begins in the foreknowledge of Yahuah regarding Yahushua being his *logos* (word) to man; that is, to reveal who the Father is through a man who never sinned. The Father moved in him so fully that Yahushua could say:

"Anyone who has seen me has seen the Father" (Jn 14:9).

And his prayer was that we be one with the Father in the same way that he is (Jn 17:21-23).

All of the Gospels select and arrange material according to their individual portrayals of Yahushua, with the order of events secondary. Of course, they all end with Yahushua's arrest, impalement, burial, resurrection and ascension. His death paid the penalty for our sin, and his resurrection and ascension vindicated that what he did guaranteed salvation for us. The end of John states how the selection was done in that book.

"There were indeed many other signs that Yahushua did in the presence of his disciples which are not written in this book, 31 *but these are written so that you believe that Yahushua is the Messiah, the Son of Elohim, and that believing you might possess life in his name"* (Jn 20:30-31).

Here are a few quotes from each of the Gospels.

Matthew

Mt 5:3. *"Blessed are the poor in spirit, because theirs is the kingdom of the heavens."*

Mt 6:21. *"Where your treasure is, there also shall be your heart."*

Mt 6:33. *"Seek first the kingdom of Elohim and his righteousness, and all these things shall be added to you."*

Mt 7:1. *"Do not judge, lest you be judged."*

7:14. *"The gate is narrow and the way is hard pressed which leads to life, and there are few who find it."*

Mt 10:22. *"You shall be hated by all for my name's sake. But he who shall have endured to the end shall be saved."*

Mt 11:29. *"Take my yoke upon you and learn from me, for I am meek and humble in heart, and you shall find rest for your souls."*

Mt 12:40. *"For as Jonah was three days and three nights in the stomach of the great fish, so shall the Son of Man be three days and three nights in the heart of the earth."*

Mt 16:24. *"If anyone wishes to come after me, let him deny himself and take up his stake and follow me."*

Mark

Mk 6:4. *"A prophet is not honored except in his own country, among his own relatives and in his own house."*

Mk 9:23. *"If you are able, all is possible to him who believes."*

Mk 9:35. *"If anyone wishes to be first, he shall be last of all and servant of all."*

Mk 10:25. *"It is easier for a camel to enter through the eye of a needle than for a rich man to enter into the kingdom of Elohim."*

Mk 16:20.*And they went out and proclaimed everywhere, while the Master worked with them and confirmed the word through the accompanying signs.*

Luke

Lk 11:36. *"If then all your body is light, having no part dark, all shall be light as when the bright shining of a lamp gives you light."*

Lk 12:15. *"Mind and beware of greed, because one's life does not consist in the excess of his possessions."*

Lk 12:51. *"Do you think that I came to give peace on earth? I say to you, no, but rather division."*

Lk 17:6. *"If you have faith as a mustard seed you would say to this mulberry tree, 'Be pulled up by the roots and be planted in the sea,' and it would obey you."*

Lk 22:42. *"Father, if you are willing, remove this cup from me. Yet not my will, but yours be done."*

John

Jn 1:12. *But as many as received him, to them he gave the authority to become children of Elohim, to those believing in his name.*

Jn 3:8. *"The wind blows where it wishes and you hear the sound of it, but do not know where it comes from and where it goes. So is everyone who has been born of the spirit."*

Jn 4:34. *"My food is to do the will of him who sent me and to complete his work."*

Jn 5:19. *"Truly, truly, I say to you, the Son is able to do nothing by himself, but only that which he sees the Father doing; whatever he does, the Son also likewise does."*

Jn 5:36. *"The works that I do bear witness of me, that the Father has sent me."*

Jn 6:35. *"I am the bread of life. Whoever comes to me shall never hunger, and he who believes in me shall never thirst."*

Jn 6:44. *"No one is able to come to me unless the Father who sent me draws him."*

Jn 8:32 *"You shall know the truth, and the truth shall make you free."*

Jn 10:27. *"My sheep hear my voice, and I know them and they follow me."*

Jn 10:30. *"I and my Father are one."*

Jn 11:25. *"I am the resurrection and the life. He who believes in me, though he dies, he shall live."*

Jn 12:25. *"He who loves his life shall lose it, and he who hates his life in this world shall preserve it for everlasting life."*

Jn 14:6. *"I am the Way, and the Truth, and the Life. No one comes to the Father except through me."*

Jn 14:12. *"Truly, truly, I say to you, he who believes in me, the works that I do he shall do also. And greater works than these he shall do, because I go to my Father."*

Jn 15:16. *"You did not choose me, but I chose you and appointed you that you should go and bear fruit and that your fruit should remain, so that whatever you ask the Father in my name he might give you."*

Jn 17:23. *"I in them and you in me so that they might be perfected into one, so that the world knows that you have sent me and have loved them as you have loved me."*

Miracles of Yahushua Messiah

CHRONOLOGICAL TABLE OF
THE MIRACLES OF CHRIST, *by* DAVID BROWN

(www.ccel.org/j/jfb/jfb/JFB00F.htm) (public domain)

MIRACLES.	WHERE WROUGHT.	WHERE RECORDED.
Water made wine	Cana	Joh 2:1-11.
Nobleman's son healed	Cana	Joh 4:46-54.
First miraculous draught of fishes	Sea of Galilee	Lu 5:1-11.
Leper healed	Capernaum	Mt 8:2-4; Mark 1:40-45; Lu 5:12-15.
Centurion's servant healed	Capernaum	Mt 8:5-13; Lu 7:1-10.
Widow's son raised to life	Nain	Lu 7:11-17.
Demoniac healed	Capernaum	Mr 1:21-28; Lu 4:31-37.
Peter's mother-in-law healed	Capernaum	Mt 8:14, 15; Mr 1:29-31; Lu 4:38, 39.
Paralytic healed	Capernaum	Mt 9:2-8; Mr 2:1-12; Lu 5:17-26.
Impotent man healed	Jerusalem	Joh 5:1-16.
Man with withered hand healed	Galilee	Mt 12:10-14; Mr 3:1-6; Lu 6:6-11.
Blind and dumb demoniac healed	Galilee	Mt 12:22-24; Lu 11:14.
Tempest stilled	Sea of Galilee	Mt 8:23-27; Mr 4:35-41; Lu 8:22-25.
Demoniacs dispossessed	Gadara	Mt 8:28-34; Mr 5:1-20.
Jairus' daughter raised to life	Capernaum	Mt 9:18-26; Mr 5:22-24; Lu 8:41-56.
Issue of blood healed	Near Capernaum	Mt 9:18-26; Mr 5:22-24; Lu 8:41-56.
Two blind men restored to sight	Capernaum	Mt 9:27-31.

167

Dumb demoniac healed	Capernaum	Mt 9:32-34.
Five thousand miraculously fed	Decapolis	Mt 14:13-21; Mr 6:31-44; Lu 9:10-17; Joh 6:5-14.
Jesus walks on the sea	Sea of Galilee	Mt 14:22-33; Mr 6:45-52; Joh 6:15-21.
Syrophœnician's daughter healed	Coasts of Tyre and Sidon	Mt 15:21-28; Mr 7:24-30.
Deaf and dumb man healed	Decapolis	Mr 7:31-37.
Four thousand fed	Decapolis	Mt 15:32-39; Mr 8:1-9.
Blind man restored to sight	Bethsaida	Mr 8:22-26.
Demoniac and lunatic boy healed	Near Cæsarea Philippi	Mt 17:14-21; Mr 9:14-29; Lu 9:37-43.
Miraculous provision of tribute	Capernaum	Mt 17:24-27.
The eyes of one born blind opened	Jerusalem	Joh 9:1-41.
Woman, of eighteen years' infirmity, cured	[Perea.]	Lu 13:10-17.
Dropsical man healed	[Perea.]	Lu 14:1-6.
Ten lepers cleansed	Borders of Samaria	Lu 17:11-19.
Lazarus raised to life	Bethany	Joh 11:1-46.
Two blind beggars restored to sight	Jericho	Mt 20:29-34; Mr 10:46-52; Lu 18:35-43.
Barren fig tree blighted	Bethany	Mt 21:12, 13, 18, 19; Mr 11:12-24.
Malchus' ear healed	Gethsemane	Mt 26:51-54; Mr 14:47-49; Lu 22:50, 51; Joh 18:10,11.
Second draught of fishes	Sea of Galilee	Joh 21:1-14.

Parables of Yahushua

From Thompson Chain - Topics
In All Three Gospels
New Cloth. Matthew 9 Mark 2; Luke 5.
New Wine in Old Wineskins. Matthew 9; Mark 2; Luke 5.
The Fig Tree. Matthew 24; Mark 13; Luke 21.

The Mustard Seed. Matthew 13; Mark 4; Luke 13.
The Sower. Matthew 13; Mark 4; Luke 8.
The Wicked Farmer. Matthew 21; Mark 12; Luke 20.
In Two Gospels Only
The House on the Rock. Matthew 7; Luke 6.
The Yeast. Matthew 13; Luke 13.
The Lost Sheep. Matthew 18; Luke 15.
In one Gospel only
The Barren Fig Tree. Luke 13.
The Dragnet. Matthew 13.
The Friend at Midnight. Luke 11.
The Good Samaritan. Luke 10.
The Good Shepherd. John 10.
The Fine Pearl. Matthew 13.
The Great Supper. Luke 14.
The Hidden Treasure. Matthew 13.
The Householder. Mark 13.
The Laborers in the Vineyard. Matthew 20.
The Marriage Feast for King's Son. Matthew 22.
The Pharisee and Tax-gatherer. Luke 18.
The Pieces of Money. Luke 15.
The Pounds. Luke 19.
The Prodigal Son. Luke 15.
The Rich Fool Luke 12.
The Rich Man and Lazarus. Luke 16.
The Seed Growing in Secret. Mark 4.
The Sheep and Goats. Matthew 25.
The Tares. Matthew 13.
The Ten Talents. Matthew 25.
The Ten Virgins. Matthew 25.
The Two Debtors. Luke 7.
The Two Sons. Matthew 21.
The Unjust Judge. Luke 18.
The Unjust Steward. Luke 16.
The Unmerciful Servant. Matthew 18.
The Unprofitable Servants. Luke 17.
The Wedding Feast. Luke 12.
The Wise Steward. Luke 12.
—Thompson Chain – Topics.

5. Acts of the Apostles

This book is a sequel to Luke and has often been referred to as "The Acts of the Holy Spirit." The Gospel of Luke ends with telling the disciples to wait in Jerusalem for the Promise of the Father, which is the set-apart spirit. The beginning of Acts has this commission to the disciples, a commission which is played out as an outline of the book.

> *"But you shall receive power when the set-apart spirit has come upon you, and you shall be my witnesses in Jerusalem and in all Judea and Samaria and to the end of the earth"* (Ac 1:8).

They received that power at Pentecost (Act 2). Peter became the apostle to the Jews, but he also opened the door to the gentiles (Act 10). And Paul, after his conversion, became the apostle to the gentiles. The book records his three missionary journeys, plus his trip as a prisoner to Rome.

It should be noted that the book of Acts is the only book in the scriptures that shows what happens when people receive the set-apart spirit. The common sign of having received is speaking in tongues; that is, a language unknown to the one speaking. Here is the account in Acts 10.

> *And those of the circumcision* (Jews) *who believed were astonished, as many as came with Peter, because the gift of the set-apart spirit had been poured out on the gentiles also, for they were hearing them speaking with tongues and extolling Elohim.*
>
> *Then Peter answered, "Is anyone able to forbid water that these should not be immersed* (in water) *who have received the set-apart spirit—even as we also?"* (Referring to speaking in tongues on the day of Pentecost.) (Ac 10:45-47).

Even as Yahushua did miracles, signs and wonders to confirm his message, so did the apostles.

- Peter heals a lame man (Act 3).
- Peter's shadow heals people, and Ananias and his wife Sapphira drop dead when lying (Act 5).
- Philip is transported supernaturally to a different location (Act 8).
- Peter heals a bedridden paralytic and raises a woman from the dead (Act. 9).
- A heavenly messenger takes Peter out of prison (Act 12).
- Paul heals a man who was crippled at birth (Act 14).
- Paul casts out a demon spirit (Act 16).
- Handkerchiefs and aprons are used to heal the sick and cast out

demons (Act 19).
- Paul raises a young man from death (Act 20).
- Paul unhurt when bitten by a poisonous snake (Act 28).

Besides these specific miracles, general statements are made about healing.

> Ac 2:43. *And fear came upon every being, and many wonders and signs were being done through the apostles.*

> Ac 4:31. *And when they had prayed the place where they came together was shaken. And they were all filled with the set-apart spirit and they spoke the word of Elohim with boldness.*

> Ac 5:16. *A large number also gathered from the surrounding cities to Jerusalem, bringing sick ones and those who were troubled by unclean spirits, and they were all healed.*

> Ac 14:3. *So they remained a long time speaking boldly in the Master, who was bearing witness to the word of his favor, giving signs and wonders to be done by their hands.*

Acts also records many instances of believers being persecuted. The first martyr was Stephen. He had a vision of Yahushua standing at the right hand of Elohim, and was stoned to death (Act 7). In fact, it was persecution in Jerusalem that led to believers going to other cities and proclaiming the good news in those places.

The book of Acts is a picture of what the assembly of Yahushua is supposed to look like; that is, operating in the power and leading of the spirit with signs and wonders to confirm the message. The assembly has fallen far from that pattern, just as Israel fell far from the Torah/Law given at Sinai. But the promise of restoration for Israel in the last days also applies to the assembly, and it will be fulfilled in the last-day perfected bride of Messiah.

NINE LETTERS TO ASSEMBLIES

For a summary of the letters see the "Brief Survey of the 66 Books" earlier in this book. Included here are a few quotes from the letters. First, however, we have an analysis of all the New Testament scriptures from Easton's Bible Dictionary, giving the author, when written, and some remarks, such as where written. Letters written in Rome were when Paul was in prison. The three letters to assemblies written in Rome are also referred to as the Prison Epistles.

Name	Written By	A.D.	Remarks
Matthew	Matthew	50-60	Aramaic/Greek
Mark	Mark	63-70	At Rome (directed by Peter)
Luke	Luke	58-60	Caesarea
John	John	78	Ephesus
Acts	Luke	63	
Romans	Paul	58	Corinth
1 Corinthians	Paul	57	Ephesus
2 Corinthians	Paul	58	Philippi
Galatians	Paul	54	Ephesus
Ephesians	Paul	62	Rome (while in prison)
Philippians	Paul	62	Rome (while in prison)
Colossians	Paul	62	Rome (while in prison)
1 Thessalonians	Paul	53	Corinth
2 Thessalonians	Paul	53	Corinth
1 Timothy	Paul	67	Macedonia
2 Timothy	Paul	68	Rome (while in prison)
Titus	Paul	67	Ephesus
Philemon	Paul	62	Rome
Hebrews	Paul	58	Corinth (Hebrew/Greek)
James	James	45-62	Jesus' brother
1 Peter	Peter	60-67	Babylon
2 Peter	Peter		
1 John	John	78	Ephesus
2 John	John	78	
3 John	John	78	
Jude	Judas	60-67	Brother of James
Revelation	John	89-99	In Patmos

from Easton's Bible Dictionary

1. Romans

DATE WRITTEN: A.D. 57 near the end of his third missionary journey. Evidently written from Corinth.

PURPOSE: To prepare the believers of Rome for his long awaited visit. He wanted to spiritually edify them and also establish his apostolic authority through a foundational theological treatise.

—Thompson Chain - Bible Book Outlines

Ro 1:20. *For since the creation of the world his invisible qualities have been clearly seen, being understood from what has been made, both his everlasting power and mightiness, for them* to be without excuse.

Ro 2:13. *For not the hearers of the law are righteous in the sight of Elohim, but the doers of the law shall be declared right.*

Ro 3:10. *As it has been written, "There is none righteous, no, not one!"*

Ro 5:8. *But Elohim proves his own love for us, in that while we were still sinners Messiah died for us.*

Ro 5:9. *Much more then, having now been declared right by his blood, we shall be saved from wrath through him.*

Ro 6:11. *So you also reckon yourselves to be dead indeed to sin, but alive to Elohim in Messiah Yahushua our Master.*

Ro 6:16. *Do you not know that … you are servants of the one whom you obey, whether of sin to death, or of obedience to righteousness?*

Ro 8:9. *But you are not in the flesh but in the spirit, if indeed the spirit of Elohim dwells in you. And if anyone does not have the spirit of Messiah, this one is not his.*

Ro 8:14. *For as many as are led by the spirit of Elohim, these are sons of Elohim.*

Ro 8:29. *Because those whom he knew beforehand he also ordained beforehand to be conformed to the likeness of his Son, for him to be the first-born among many brothers.*

Ro 10:9. *That if you confess with your mouth the Master Yahushua and believe in your heart that Elohim has raised him from the dead, you shall be saved.* 10 *For with the heart one believes to righteousness, and confesses with the mouth to salvation.*

Ro 12:2. *And do not be conformed to this world system, but be transformed by the renewing of your mind, so that you prove what is that good and well-pleasing and perfect desire of Elohim.*

2. First Corinthians

The assembly in Corinth had problems with division, with immorality, with the authority of Paul as the apostle who founded their assembly, and with understanding the nature of the Lord's Supper or communion, the operation of the gifts of the spirit, and the resurrection of the dead. Paul addresses these and other issues in this letter.

1Cor 1:10. *And I appeal to you, brothers, by the name of our Master Yahushua Messiah, that you all agree and that there be no divisions among you, but that you be knit together in the same mind and in the same opinion.*

1Cor 2:11. *For who among men knows the thoughts of a man except the spirit of the man that is in him? So also, the thoughts of Elohim no one has known except the spirit of Elohim.*

1Cor 2:14. *But the natural man does not receive the matters of the spirit of Elohim for they are foolishness to him, and he is unable to know them because they are spiritually discerned.*

1Cor 3:19. *For the wisdom of this world system is foolishness with Elohim. For it has been written, "He catches the wise in their craftiness."*

1Cor 4:20. *The kingdom of Elohim is not in speech but in power.*

1Cor 6:9-10. *Do you not know that the unrighteous shall not inherit the kingdom of Elohim? Do not be deceived. Neither those who do sex outside of marriage, homosexuals, nor thieves, nor greedy of gain, nor drunkards, nor revilers, nor swindlers shall inherit the reign of Elohim.*

1Cor 8:6. *For us there is one Elohim, the Father, from whom all came and for whom we live, and one Master Yahushua Messiah, through whom all came and through whom we live.*

1Cor 10:13. *No trial has overtaken you except such as is common to man, and Elohim is trustworthy who will not allow you to be tried beyond what you are able, but with the trial shall also make the way of escape so you can bear it.*

1Cor 10:31. *Therefore, whether you eat or drink or whatever you do, do all to the esteem of Elohim.*

1Cor 12:7. *And to each one is given the outward showing of the spirit for profiting the assembly.*

1Cor 12:28. *And Elohim has appointed these in the assembly: first apostles, second prophets, third teachers, after that miracles, then gifts of healings, helps, ministrations, kinds of tongues.*

1Cor 13:8. *Love never fails.*

1Cor 14:1. *Pursue love and earnestly seek the spiritual things* (gifts), *but rather that you prophesy.*

1Cor 15:51. *See, I speak a secret to you: We shall not all sleep* (die), *but we shall all be changed,* [52] *in a moment, in the twinkling of an eye, at the last trumpet. For the trumpet shall sound and the dead shall be raised incorruptible, and we shall be changed.*

3. Second Corinthians

PURPOSE: To expose "deceitful workers" and to defend Paul's apostolic authority.

MAIN THEME: This is somewhat hidden, but it is quite apparent that Paul had in mind the vindication of his apostleship when he wrote this book. Both epistles to the Corinthians indicate that there was an element in this church that tended to discredit his ministry and authority.

—Thompson Chain - Bible Book Outlines

2Cor 3:18. *And we all, as with unveiled face, see as in a mirror the esteem of Yahuah; and we are being transformed into the same likeness from esteem to esteem, as from Yahuah, the spirit.*

2Cor 4:7. *And we have this treasure in earthen vessels, so that the excellence of the power might be of Elohim and not of us .*

2Cor 4:16. *Therefore we do not lose heart, but even if our outward man is perishing, the inward man is being renewed day by day.*

2Cor 4:17. *For this slight momentary pressure is working for us a far more exceeding and everlasting weight of esteem.*

2Cor 5:10. *For we all must appear before the judgment seat of Messiah, in order for each one to receive according to what he has done in the body, whether good or evil.*

2Cor 5:14. *For the love of Messiah compels us, having concluded this: that if one died for all, then all died;* [15] *and he died for all, that those who live should no longer live for themselves, but for him who died for them and was raised.*

2Cor 5:21. *For he made him who knew no sin to be sin* (offering) *for us, so that in him we might become the righteousness of Elohim.*

2Cor 6:14. *Do not become unevenly yoked with unbelievers. For what partnership have righteousness and lawlessness? And what fellowship has light with darkness? ...*

2Cor 6:17. *Therefore, "Come out from among them and be*

separate, says Yahuah, and do not touch what is unclean, and I shall receive you. ¹⁸ *And I shall be a Father to you and you shall be sons and daughters to me, says Yahuah Almighty."*

2Cor 11:2. *For I am jealous for you with a jealousy according to Elohim. For I gave you in marriage to one husband, to present you as an innocent maiden to Messiah.*

2Cor 12:12. *Indeed, the signs of an apostle were done among you with all endurance, in signs and wonders and powers.*

2Cor 13:5. *Examine yourselves whether you are in the faith— prove yourselves. Or do you not know yourselves that Yahushua Messiah is in you, unless you are disapproved.*

4. Galatians

PURPOSE: To defend the doctrine of justification by faith, warn against a reversion to Judaism, and vindicate Paul's own apostolic authority.

MAIN THEMES: The main argument is in favor of Christian liberty in opposition to the teachings of the Judaizers. These false teachers insisted that the observance of the ceremonial law [especially circumcision] was an essential part of the plan of salvation.

—Thompson Chain - Bible Book Outlines

Gal 2:20. *I have been impaled with Messiah, and I no longer live but Messiah lives in me. And that which I now live in the flesh I live by faith in the Son of Elohim who loved me and gave himself for me..*

Gal 3:27. *For as many of you as were immersed into Messiah have put on Messiah.*

Gal 5:1. *Stand firm, then, in the freedom with which Messiah has made us free, and do not again be held with a yoke of slavery* (the law of circumcision).

Gal 5:6. *For in Messiah Yahushua, whether being circumcised or not has any value, but faith working through love.*

Gal 5:14. *For the entire Law is completed in one word, in this, "You shall love your neighbour as yourself."*

Gal 5:16. *And I say: Walk in the spirit and you shall not at all* (Gk double negative) *accomplish the desire of the flesh.*

Gal 5:22-23,25. *But the fruit of the spirit is love, joy, peace, patience, kindness, goodness, trustworthiness, gentleness, self-control. Against such there is no law. ... If we live in the spirit let us also walk in the spirit.*

Gal 6:7. *Do not be led astray: Elohim is not mocked, for whatever a man sows, that he shall also reap.*

5. Ephesians

MAIN THEME: The converted Jews in the early churches were inclined to be exclusive and to separate themselves from their Gentile brethren. This condition in the church at Ephesus may have been the historical occasion which led to the writing of this epistle. For this is the keynote of the book—the unity of the church, especially between Jew and Gentile believers. This is shown by the recurrence of such words and phrases as:

(1) Together: made alive together,--Ephesians 2:5; raised up together, sitting together,--Ephesians 2:6; built together,--Ephesians 2:22.

(2) One, indicating unity: one new man,--Ephesians 2:15; one body,--Ephesians 2:16; one Spirit,--Ephesians 2:18; one hope, 4:4; one Lord, one faith, one baptism, one God and Father of all,--Ephesians 4:5-6.

—Thompson Chain - Bible Book Outlines

Eph 2:8. *For by favor you have been saved, through belief and that not of yourselves; it is the gift of Elohim,* ⁹ *not by works, lest anyone should boast.* ¹⁰ *For we are his workmanship, created in Messiah Yahushua for good works which Elohim prepared beforehand that we should walk in them.*

Eph 3:19. *to know the love of Messiah which surpasses knowledge, in order that you might be filled to all the completeness of Elohim.*

Eph 4:1. *I call upon you therefore, I the prisoner of the Master, to walk worthily of the calling with which you were called,* ² *with all humility and meekness, with patience, bearing with one another in love.*

Eph 4:11. *And he gave some as apostles, and some as prophets, and some as evangelists, and some as pastors and teachers,* ¹² *for the equipping of the set-apart ones for the work of service to the building up of the body of Messiah,* ¹³ *until we all come to the unity of the faith and of the knowledge of the Son of Elohim, to a completed man, to the measure of the stature of the fullness of Messiah.*

Eph 4:22. *With regard to your former way of life, put off the old man being corrupted according to the deceitful desires, 23 and be renewed in the spirit of your mind* [the way that you think].

Eph 5:8. *For you were once darkness, but now you are light in the Master. Walk as children of light 9(for the fruit of the spirit is in all goodness and righteousness and truth) 10 proving* [by your life] *what is well-pleasing to the Master. 11 And have no fellowship with the unfruitful works of darkness, but rather reprove them.*

Eph 5:27. *that* (Messiah) *might present to himself the assembly in all her esteem, having no spot or wrinkle or any such thing, but that she would be set-apart and blameless.*

Eph 6:11. *Put on the complete armor of Elohim for you to have power to stand against the schemes of the devil.*

6. Philippians

PURPOSE: To express Paul's affection for the believers in Philippi, thank them for their gift, and encourage them to a lifestyle of unity, holiness, and joy.

SYNOPSIS: This is a spiritual love letter to the church. It contains outbursts of warm affection and gratitude. Written under hard circumstances, while Paul was a prisoner, he strikes the keynotes of victory and joy.

—Thompson Chain - Bible Book Outlines

Php 1:6. *Being persuaded of this, that he who has begun a good work in you shall complete it until the day of Yahushua Messiah.*

Php 1:29. *Because to you it has been given, on behalf of Messiah, not only to believe into him, but also to suffer for his sake.*

Php 2:4. *Each one should look out not only for his own interests, but also for the interests of others.*

Php 2:12. *Therefore, my beloved, as you always obeyed—not only in my presence but now much more in my absence—work out your own salvation with fear and trembling, 13 for it is Elohim who is working in you, both to desire and to work for his good pleasure.*

Php 3:10. *To know him and the power of his resurrection and the fellowship of his sufferings, being conformed to his death,* [11] *if somehow I might attain to the resurrection from the dead* (referring to the rapture). [12] *Not that I have already received or already been completed, but I pursue to possess that for which Messiah Yahushua has also pursued me.* [13] *Brothers, I do not count myself to have attained it yet, but only this: forgetting what is behind and reaching out for what lies ahead,* [14] *I press on toward the goal for the prize of the high calling* (upward call) *of Elohim in Messiah Yahushua.*

Php 3:20. *For our citizenship is in heaven, from which we also eagerly wait for the savior Master Yahushua Messiah* (the rapture).

Php 4:4. *Rejoice in Yahuah always; again I say, rejoice!*

Php 4:13. *I have strength to do all things through Messiah who empowers me.*

7. Colossians

MAIN THEMES: The epistle resembles Ephesians, both in thought and language, yet has a distinct message of its own. In Ephesians Paul dwells on the thought of the church as the body of Christ, while in Colossians he emphasizes Christ as the head of the church. The warning against trusting in worldly wisdom that appears in 1 Corinthians reappears in Colossians.
—Thompson Chain - Bible Book Outlines

Col 1:10. *to walk worthily of the Master, pleasing all, bearing fruit in every good work and increasing in the knowledge of Elohim, ...* [13] *who has delivered us from the authority of darkness and transferred us into the kingdom of the Son of his love* [14] *in whom we have redemption through his* (the Son's) *blood, the forgiveness of sins,* [15] *who is the likeness of the invisible Elohim, the first-born of all creation.*

Col 2:9. *Because in him bodily lives the fullness of all that Elohim is.*

Col 2:13. *And you, being dead in your trespasses ...,* Elohim *has made alive together with* Yahushua, *having forgiven you all trespasses,* [14] *having blotted out the certificate of debt against us—by the dogmas—which stood against us. And* Elohim *has taken it out of the way, having nailed it to the stake.*

Col 3:4. *When the Messiah, who is our life, is manifested, then you also shall be manifested with him in esteem.*

Col 3:16. *Let the word of Messiah dwell in you richly, teaching and admonishing one another in all wisdom, singing with pleasure in your hearts to the Master in psalms and songs of praise and spiritual songs.* 17 *And whatever you do in word or deed, do all in the name of the Master Yahushua, giving thanks to Elohim the Father through him.*

Col 3:23. *And whatever you do, do it heartily as to the Master and not to men,* 24 *knowing that from the Master you shall receive the reward of the inheritance. It is the Master Messiah you serve.*

8. First Thessalonians

DATE WRITTEN: Time and place are uncertain. It is generally thought that this was the earliest of Paul's epistles and was probably written from Corinth between A.D. 49 and 54. Paul had sent Timothy to encourage and strengthen the church. On his return, the report that he gave apparently inspired the apostle to write the epistle (1 Thessalonians 3:6).

PURPOSE: To comfort believers and encourage them to a life of purity by expounding on the doctrine of Christ's imminent return.

TO WHOM WRITTEN: The church in Thessalonica. It had been founded by Paul on his second missionary journey. He met with violent opposition in his work, but he succeeded in winning some Jews and a multitude of Greeks, which enabled him to establish a faithful church (Acts 17:1-10).

MAIN THEMES: This is one of the most personal of all of Paul's epistles. It is not so doctrinal or polemical as some of the others. The body of the epistle consists chiefly of commendations, personal reminiscences, counsels, and exhortations. The central truth that is emphasized is the future hope of the advent of Christ.

—Thompson Chain - Bible Book Outlines

1Th 1:5 *Because our Good News did not come to you in word only, but also in power and in the set-apart spirit and in entire confirmation, as you know what kind of men we were among you for your sake.*

1Th 4:7. *For Elohim did not call us to uncleanness, but in set-apartness.*

1Th 4:14. *For if we believe that Yahushua died and rose again, so also Elohim shall bring with him those who sleep in Yahushua.* ¹⁵ *For this we say to you by the word of the Master, that we, the living who are left over at the coming of the Master, shall in no way go before those who are asleep.* ¹⁶ *Because the Master himself shall come down from heaven with a shout, with the voice of a chief messenger, and with the trumpet of Elohim, and the dead in Messiah shall rise first.* ¹⁷ *Then we, the living who are left over, shall be caught away together with them in the clouds to meet the Master in the air, and so we shall always be with the Master.* ¹⁸ *So, then, encourage one another with these words.*

This is the foundation passage for the doctrine or teaching of the rapture.

1Th 5:2 *For you yourselves know very well that the day of Yahuah comes as a thief in the night.* ³ *For when they say, "Peace and safety!" then suddenly destruction comes upon them as labor pains upon a pregnant woman, and they shall not escape.* ⁴ *But you, brothers, are not in darkness so that this day should overtake you as a thief.* ⁵ *For you are all sons of light and sons of the day. We are not of the night nor of darkness.* ⁶ *So, then, we should not sleep as others do, but we should watch and be sober.*

1Th 5:23. *And the Elohim of peace himself set you completely apart, and your entire spirit and the being and the body be preserved blameless at the coming of our Master Yahushua Messiah!* ²⁴ *He who calls you is trustworthy who also shall do it.*

9. Second Thessalonians

PURPOSE: It is apparent that certain expressions in Paul's first epistle to this church had been misinterpreted. When he had referred to the uncertainty of the time of Christ's coming, his words had been understood as teaching that the day of the Lord had come (2 Thessalonians 2:2).

This resulted in undue excitement. The converts were "shaken in [their] mind," (2 Thessalonians 2:2). They were entertaining wrong views as to the nearness of the Lord's advent which unsettled their lives. Paul's purpose was to correct this perspective.
—Thompson Chain - Bible Book Outlines

2Th 2:3. *Let no one deceive you in any way, because the falling away is to come first and* [after the rapture, vs. 2:8] *the man of lawlessness is to be revealed, the son of destruction.*

2Th 3:13. *And you, brothers, do not grow weary in doing good.*

THREE PASTORAL LETTERS

T HESE THREE LETTERS give instructions on being a pastor.

1. First Timothy

PURPOSE: To encourage Timothy, Paul's young assistant, to be a godly example (1 Timothy 4:12), exercising his spiritual gifts (1 Timothy 4:14); and to give guidance in his pastoral responsibilities during Paul's absence (1 Timothy 3:14-15).
MAIN THEMES: Advice and exhortation to a young pastor respecting his personal conduct and ministerial work.
—Thompson Chain - Bible Book Outlines

1Ti 1:17. *Now to the Sovereign of the ages, incorruptible, invisible, to Elohim who alone is wise, be respect and esteem forever and ever. Amen.*

1Ti 2:5. *For there is one Elohim, and one mediator between Elohim and men, the man Messiah Yahushua.*

1Ti 3:2. *An overseer, then, should be blameless, the husband of one wife, sober, sensible, orderly, kind to strangers, able to teach.*

1Ti 4:1. *But the spirit distinctly says that in latter times some shall fall away from the faith, paying attention to misleading spirits and teachings of demons,*

1Ti 4:14. *Do not neglect the gift that is in you which was given to you by prophecy with the laying on of the hands of the elders.*

1Ti 5:8. *And if anyone does not provide for his own and especially for those of his household, he has denied the faith and is worse than an unbeliever.*

1Ti 6:12. *Fight the good fight of the faith, lay hold on everlasting life to which you were also called and have confessed the good confession before many witnesses.*

1Ti 6:16. *[Elohim] alone has immortality, dwelling in unapproachable light, whom no one has seen or is able to see, to whom be respect and everlasting strength. Amen.*

2. Second Timothy

PURPOSE:

(1) General, to encourage and instruct a young pastor in his ministerial work.

(2) Special, to request Timothy, his son in the Gospel, to hasten to Rome so that Paul might have the comfort of his companionship,--2 Timothy 1:4; 4:9, 21.

MAIN THEMES: Faithfulness and boldness in the ministry, especially in the face of opposition and suffering.

—Thompson Chain - Bible Book Outlines

2Ti 1:6. *For this reason I remind you to stir up the gift of Elohim which is in you through the laying on of my hands. 7 For Elohim has not given us a spirit of cowardice, but of power and of love and of self-control.*

2Ti 1:12. *For this reason I also suffer these things, but I am not ashamed; for I know whom I have believed and am persuaded that he is able to watch over that which I have entrusted to him until that day.*

2Ti 2:3. *Suffer hardship with us as a good soldier of Yahushua Messiah.*

2Ti 2:11. *Trustworthy is the word: For if we died with him, we shall also live with him. 12 If we endure, we shall also reign with him. If we deny him, he also shall deny us.*

2Ti 2:15. *Do your utmost to present yourself approved to Elohim, a worker who does not need to be ashamed, rightly handling the word of truth.*

2Ti 3:12. *And indeed, all those wishing to live reverently in Messiah Yahushua shall be persecuted.*

2Ti 3:16. *All scripture is Elohim-breathed and profitable for teaching, for reproof, for setting straight, for instruction in righteousness, 17 that the man of Elohim might be fitted, equipped for every good work.*

3. Titus

DATE WRITTEN: About A.D. 64, shortly after 1 Timothy was written.

PURPOSE: To counsel and exhort Titus, a young pastor, relating to his ministerial duties and doctrines, with special emphasis on the maintenance of good works.

TO WHOM WRITTEN: Titus. He was a Gentile (Galatians 2:3); a beloved friend and helper of Paul (2 Corinthians 2:13;7:6, 13;8:23). A messenger of the church at Corinth (2 Corinthians 8:16-18). He was thoroughly trustworthy and unselfish (2 Corinthians 12:18). A companion of Paul and Barnabas on a journey to Jerusalem (Galatians 2:1). He was left in Crete by Paul to superintend the churches (Titus 1:5). He was in Rome with Paul during the latter's imprisonment (2 Timothy 4:10).

—Thompson Chain - Bible Book Outlines

Tit 1:15. *Indeed, all things are clean to the clean, but to those who are defiled and unbelieving nothing is clean, but both their mind and conscience are defiled.* 16 *They profess to know Elohim, but in works they deny him, being abominable and disobedient and unfit for any good work.*

Tit 3:5. *He saved us, not by works of righteousness which we have done, but according to his compassion through the washing of rebirth and renewal by the set-apart spirit.*

ONE PERSONAL LETTER

THE PASTORAL LETTERS are also personal, but they are to pastors.

1. Philemon

PURPOSE: To appeal to Philemon to receive, forgive and restore Onesimus even as he [Philemon] would receive Paul.

TO WHOM WRITTEN: Philemon. He was apparently a member of the church at Colosse, which seems to have held its assemblies in his house (Philemon 1:2). His benevolence (Philemon 1:5-7), and Paul's request for him to prepare a lodging (Philemon 1:22), indicate that he was a man of some means.

As Paul had never been in Colosse (Colossians 2:1), Philemon must have met him elsewhere, possibly in Ephesus, which was not far away. It would seem that he owed his conversion to the apostle (Philemon 1:19).

MAIN THEME: A personal plea with Philemon to forgive and restore Onesimus, his once runaway slave, now converted through the ministry of Paul. As a runaway slave, it is inferred that he robbed his master and fled to Rome (Philemon 1:18). There he came under the influence of Paul and was converted (Philemon 1:10). He became a devoted disciple of Christ (Colossians

4:9). Paul would have chosen to detain him in Rome as a helper (Philemon 1:13), but not having the consent of Philemon (Philemon 1:14), he felt it to be his duty to send the slave back to his master. So the apostle writes this beautiful letter of intercession, pleading with Philemon to receive Onesimus as though he were receiving the apostle himself.

—Thompson Chain - Bible Book Outlines

Phm 1:14. *But without your consent I decided to do nothing so that your good deed should not be by way of necessity, but voluntary.*

ONE ANONOMOUS LETTER

1. Hebrews

AUTHOR: Uncertain. The epistle has been ascribed to Paul, Barnabas, Luke, Apollos, and various other persons. The most that can be said is that the weight of opinion seems to favor the Pauline authorship.

DATE WRITTEN: Uncertain, but probably before A.D. 70 when Jerusalem's Temple was destroyed. The book highlights the sacrificial ceremonies of the Temple and there is no mention of its demise.

PURPOSE: The chief doctrinal purpose of the writer was to show the transcendent glory of the Christian dispensation, as compared with that of the Old Testament.

TO WHOM WRITTEN: Hebrew Christians. These converts were in constant danger of relapsing into Judaism, or at least of attaching too much importance to ceremonial observances.

MAIN THEME: The superiority of Christ and His work.

—Thompson Chain - Bible Book Outlines

Heb 2:18. *For in what he had suffered, himself being tested, he is able to help those who are tested.*

Heb 3:14. *For we have become partakers of Messiah, if we hold fast the beginning of our trust firm to the end.*

Heb 4:9. *So there remains a sabbath-keeping for the people of Elohim.*

Heb 4:12. *For the word of Elohim is living and working and sharper than any two-edged sword, cutting through even to the dividing of soul and spirit and of joints and marrow, and able to judge the thoughts and intentions of the heart .*

Heb 5:8. *Though being a Son he learned obedience by what he suffered.* ⁹ *And having been completed, he became the source of everlasting salvation to all those obeying him.*

Heb 9:13. *For if the blood of bulls and goats and the ashes of a heifer, sprinkling the defiled, sets apart for the cleansing of the flesh,* ¹⁴ *how much more shall the blood of the Messiah, who through the everlasting spirit offered himself unblemished to Elohim, cleanse your conscience from dead works to serve the living Elohim?*

Heb 10:14. *For by one offering he has perfected for all time those who are being set apart.*

Heb 10:23. *Let us hold fast the confession of our hope without yielding, for he who promised is trustworthy.*

Heb 10:31. *It is fearsome to fall into the hands of the living Elohim.*

Heb 10:36. *For you have need of endurance, so that when you have done the desire of Elohim you receive the promise.*

Heb 11:1. *And faith is the substance of what is expected, the proof of what is not seen. ...* ⁶ *But without faith it is impossible to please him, for he who comes to Elohim must believe that he is and that he is a rewarder of those who earnestly seek him.*

Heb 12:3. *For consider him who endured such opposition from sinners against himself, lest you become weary and faint in your lives.* ⁴ *You have not yet resisted unto blood striving against sin. ...* ⁷ *If you endure discipline, Elohim is treating you as sons. For what son is there whom a father does not discipline?*

Heb 12:29. *Our Elohim is a consuming fire.*

Heb 13:5. *Let your way of life be without the love of money, and be satisfied with what you have. For he himself has said, "I shall never leave you nor forsake you,"*

Heb 13:17. *Obey those who have authority over you and be subject to them, for they watch for your lives as having to give account. Let them do so with joy and not groaning, for that would be of no advantage to you.*

SEVEN GENERAL LETTERS

1. James

AUTHOR: Uncertain. There are three prominent persons named James in the New Testament. It is generally agreed that James, called by Paul "the Lord's brother" (Galatians 1:19), was the writer of the epistle.

DATE WRITTEN: Possibly the earliest New Testament book written. Many feel it should be dated before A.D. 49, since the issues of the famous Council in Jerusalem of that year are not mentioned.

PURPOSE: To challenge believers to possess an active faith which will produce real changes in a person's conduct and character.

TO WHOM WRITTEN: Apparently addressed to the Jewish converts who lived outside the Holy Land; possibly also to the devout Jews of the dispersion,--James 1:1.

MAIN THEME: Practical religion, manifesting itself in good works, contrasted with mere profession of faith.

KEY WORDS: Faith and works,--James 2:17.

—Thompson Chain - Bible Book Outlines

Jam 1:2 *My brothers, count it all joy when you fall into various trials,* 3 *knowing that the proving of your faith works endurance.* 4 *And let endurance have a complete work, so that you be complete and whole lacking nothing.*

Jam 1:12. *Blessed is the man who endures trial, for when he has been proved he shall receive the victor's wreath of life which the Master has promised to those who love him.* 13 *Let no one say when he is tempted, "I am tempted by Elohim," for Elohim is not tempted by evil and he tempts no one.*

Jam 1:22. *Become doers of the word and not hearers only, deceiving yourselves.*

Jam 2:10. *For whoever shall guard all the Law and yet stumble in one point, he is guilty of all.*

Jam 2:19. *You believe that Elohim is one. You do well. The demons also believe, and shudder!*

Jam 2:26. *For as the body without the spirit is dead, so also faith without the works is dead.*

Jam 4:3. *You ask and do not receive because you ask evilly, in order to spend it on your pleasures.* ⁴ *Adulterers and adulteresses! Do you not know that friendship with the world is hostility with Elohim? Whoever, therefore, intends to be a friend of the world makes himself an enemy of Elohim.*

Jam 4:7. *So then, subject yourselves to Elohim. Resist the devil and he shall flee from you.* ⁸ *Draw near to Elohim and he will draw near to you. Cleanse hands, sinners, and purify the hearts, you double-minded! ...* ¹⁰ *Humble yourselves in the sight of the Master, and he shall lift you up.*

Jam 4:17. *To him, then, who knows to do good and does not do it, to him it is sin.*

Jam 5:14. *Is anyone among you sick? Let him call for the elders of the assembly, and let them pray over him having anointed him with oil in the name of the Master.* ¹⁵ *And the prayer of belief shall save the sick and the Master shall raise him up. And if he has committed sins* [if sin is involved in the sickness] *he shall be forgiven* [assuming the person has repented]. ¹⁶ *Confess your sins to one another and pray for one another so that you are healed. The earnest prayer of a righteous one accomplishes much.*

2. First Peter

MAIN THEME: Victory over suffering as exemplified in the life of Christ [and also because of the promise of Messiah's return].
—Thompson Chain - Bible Book Outlines

1Pe 1:2. *chosen according to the foreknowledge of Elohim the Father, set apart by the spirit to obedience and sprinkling of the blood of Yahushua Messiah.*

1Pe 1:5. *who are protected by the power of Elohim through belief for a deliverance ready to be revealed in the last time* [on the new earth].

1Pe 1:13. *Therefore, having girded up the loins of your mind, being sober, set your hope perfectly upon the favor that is to be brought to you at the revelation of Yahushua Messiah* [referring to the rapture].

1Pe 1:18. *knowing that you were redeemed from your futile way of life inherited from your fathers, not with what is corruptible, silver or gold,* ¹⁹ *but with the precious blood of*

Messiah, as of a lamb unblemished and spotless.

1Pe 1:23. *having been born again—not of corruptible seed, but incorruptible—through the living word of Elohim, which remains forever.*

1Pe 2:2. *As newborn babies desire the unpolluted milk of the word, in order that you grow by it.*

1Pe 2:5. *You also, as living stones, are being built up, a spiritual house, a set-apart priesthood, to offer up spiritual slaughter offerings acceptable to Elohim through Yahushua Messiah.*

1Pe 2:12. *having your behavior among the gentiles good, so that when they speak against you as evil-doers, let them esteem Elohim in a day of visitation by observing your good works.*

1Pe 2:21. *For to this you were called, because Messiah also suffered for us leaving us an example, that you should follow his steps.*

1Pe 3:15. *But set Yahuah Elohim apart in your hearts and always be ready, with humility and fear, to give an answer to everyone asking you a reason concerning the hope that is in you.*

1Pe 4:1. *Therefore, since Messiah suffered in the flesh, arm yourselves also with the same mind, because he who has suffered in the flesh has ceased from sin.*

1Pe 4:12. *Beloved ones, do not be surprised at the fiery trial that is coming upon you to try you, as though something unusual has befallen you;* ¹³ *but as you share Messiah's sufferings, rejoice, in order that you might rejoice exultingly at the revelation of his esteem.*

1Pe 4:18. *And if the righteous one is scarcely saved, where shall the wicked and the sinner appear?* ¹⁹ *So then, those who suffer according to the desire of Elohim should, in doing good, commit their lives to a trustworthy creator.*

1Pe 5:8 *Be sober, watch, because your adversary the devil walks about like a roaring lion seeking someone to devour.* ⁹ *Resist him, firm in the faith, knowing that the same hardships are experienced by your brothers in the world.*

3. Second Peter

PURPOSE: To warn believers of the dangerous and seductive work of false teachers; and to encourage them to "grow in the grace and knowledge of our Lord and Savior Jesus Christ," (2 Peter 3:18).

MAIN THEME: A warning against corrupt teachers and scoffers. In order to counteract the influence of false doctrine, great emphasis is laid upon the Word of God and the certainty of the fulfillment of the divine promises.

—Thompson Chain - Bible Book Outlines

2Pe 1:4. *Through these there have been given to us exceedingly great and precious promises, so that through these you might be partakers of a nature like Elohim, having escaped from the corruption in the world caused by lust. 5 And for this reason do your utmost to add to your faith uprightness, to uprightness knowledge, 6 to knowledge self-control, to self-control endurance, to endurance reverence, 7 to reverence brotherly affection, and to brotherly affection love. 8 For if these are in you and increase, they cause you to be neither inactive nor without fruit in the knowledge of our Master Yahushua Messiah.*

2Pe 1:10. *For this reason, brothers, all the more do your utmost to make firm your calling and choosing, for if you are doing these matters, you shall never stumble at all, 11 for in this way an entrance into the everlasting kingdom of our Master and Saviour Yahushua Messiah shall be richly supplied to you.*

2Pe 2:1. *But there also came to be false prophets among the people, as also among you there shall be false teachers, who shall secretly bring in destructive heresies and deny the Master who bought them, bringing swift destruction on themselves.*

2Pe 2:9. *Yahuah knows how to rescue the reverent ones from trial, and to keep the unrighteous unto the day of judgment to be punished.*

2Pe 3:3. *Knowing this first: that mockers shall come in the last days with mocking, walking according to their own lusts.*

2Pe 3:10. *But the day of Yahuah shall come as a thief in the night, in which the heavens shall pass away with a great noise and the elements shall melt with intense heat and the earth and the works that are in it shall be burned up. 11 Seeing all these are to be destroyed in this way, what kind of people ought you to be in set-apart behaviour and reverence,* 12 *looking for and hastening the coming of the day of Elohim, through which the heavens shall be destroyed, being set on fire, and the elements melt with intense heat!*

4. First John

PURPOSES: The writer mentions four reasons for writing this epistle to believers:

(1) To add to their joy,--1 John 1:4.

(2) To guard them against sin,--1 John 2:1.

(3) To warn them against false teachers,--1 John 2:26.

(4) To strengthen their faith in Christ and assure them of eternal life,--1 John 5:13.

MAIN THEME: God is Life, Light, and Righteous Love. His character calls for holy living and brotherly love on the part of believers.

—Thompson Chain - Bible Book Outlines

This is a letter of love, giving Yahuah as the example of how we should love, and what will result from following that example; namely, overcoming sin in our lives.

1Jn 1:3. *We announce to you what we have seen and heard so that you too might have fellowship with us. And truly our fellowship is with the Father and with his Son Yahushua Messiah.* 4 *And we write this to you in order that your joy might be complete.* 5 *And this is the message which we have heard from him and announce to you, that Elohim is light and in him is no darkness at all.* 6 *If we say that we have fellowship with him and walk in darkness, we lie and are not doing the truth.* 7 *But if we walk in the light as he is in the light, we have fellowship with one another and the blood of Yahushua Messiah his Son cleanses us from all sin.*

1Jn 2:1. *My little children, I write this to you so that you do not sin. And if anyone sins we have an intercessor with the Father, Yahushua Messiah, a righteous one.*

1Jn 2:15. *Do not love the world nor that which is in the world. If anyone loves the world, the love of the Father is not in him.* 16 *Because all that is in the world—the desire of the flesh, the desire*

191

of the eyes, and the pride of life—is not of the Father but is of the world. ¹⁷ *And the world passes away and its desire, but the one doing the desire of Elohim remains forever.*

1Jn 3:1. *See what love the Father has given us, that we should be called children of Elohim! For this reason the world does not know us, because it did not know him.*

1Jn 3:4. *Everyone doing sin also does lawlessness, and sin is lawlessness.* ⁵ *And you know that he was manifested to take away our sins, and in him there is no sin.*

1Jn 3:8. *The one doing sin is of the devil, because the devil has sinned from the beginning. For this purpose the Son of Elohim was manifested: to destroy the works of the devil.*

1Jn 3:16. *By this we have known love, because he laid down his life for us. And we ought to lay down our lives for the brothers.*

1Jn 3:22. *And whatever we ask we receive from him because we keep his commands and do what is pleasing in his sight.*

1Jn 4:4. *You are of Elohim, little children, and have overcome them, because he who is in you is greater than he who is in the world.*

1Jn 4:8. *The one who does not love does not know Elohim, for Elohim is love.* ⁹ *By this the love of Elohim was manifested in us, that Elohim has sent his only begotten Son into the world in order that we might live through him.* ¹⁰ *In this is love, not that we loved Elohim, but that he loved us and sent his Son to be an atoning offering for our sins.*

1Jn 4:18. *There is no fear in love, but perfect love casts out fear, because fear holds punishment and he who fears has not been made perfect in love.*

1Jn 5:5. *Who is the one who overcomes the world, but he who believes that Yahushua is the Son of Elohim?*

1Jn 5:14. *And this is the boldness that we have in him, that if we ask anything according to his will, he hears us.*

5. Second John

PURPOSE: The epistle was apparently written to warn friends against heresy and association with false teachers,--2 John 1:7-11. —Thompson Chain - Bible Book Outlines

2Jn 1:9. *Everyone who is transgressing and not staying in the teaching of Messiah does not possess Elohim. The one who stays in the teaching of Messiah possesses both the Father and the Son.*

6. Third John

PURPOSES:

(1) To commend Gaius for his loyalty to the truth and for his care of traveling teachers and missionaries.

(2) To rebuke Diotrephes for his pride.

(3) To recommend Demetrius to Gaius.

(4) To inform the readers of his imminent visit.

—Thompson Chain - Bible Book Outlines

3Jn 1:11. *Beloved ones, do not imitate the evil but the good. The one who is doing good is of Elohim, but he who is doing evil has not seen Elohim.*

7. Jude

PURPOSE: The epistle was evidently written to warn the church against immoral teachers and alarming heresies which were endangering the faith of believers.

MAIN THEME: Heretical teachers in the church and the believer's godly response to that divisive threat.

KEY WORDS: Contend earnestly for the faith,--Jude 1:3.

—Thompson Chain - Bible Book Outlines

Jude 1:3. *Beloved ones, making all haste to write to you concerning our common salvation, I felt it necessary to write to you urging you to earnestly contend for the faith which was once for all delivered to the set-apart ones.* 4 *For certain men have slipped in whose judgment was written about long ago, wicked ones perverting the favor of our Elohim for indecency and denying the only Master Yahuah and our Master Yahushua Messiah.*

Jude 1:10. *But these blaspheme that which they do not know. And that which they know naturally, like unreasoning beasts, in these they corrupt themselves.* 11 *Woe to them! Because they have gone in the way of Cain and gave themselves to the delusion of Balaam for a reward and perished in the rebellion of Korah. ...* 14 *And Enoch, the seventh from Adam, also prophesied of these,* saying, *"See, Yahuah comes with his myriads of set-apart ones.*

Jude 1:20. *But you, beloved ones, building yourselves up on your most set-apart belief, praying in the set-apart spirit* [referring to praying in tongues].

Jude 1:24. *And to him who is able to keep you from stumbling and to present you blameless before the presence of his esteem with exceeding joy,* 25 *to the only wise Elohim our savior, be esteem and greatness and might and authority, both now and forever. Amen.*

ONE BOOK OF PROPHECY

ALL OF THE SCRIPTURE BOOKS are prophetic. This one, however, is especially so, for it is about the day of Yahuah.

1. Revelation/Apocalypse

PURPOSE: To give hope to Christians, especially those who suffer, by revealing Jesus Christ as the ultimate victorious King of Kings and Lord of Lords (Revelation 19:16). The book manifests its own AUTHORITY in declaring itself to be the revelation of Jesus Christ (Revelation 1:1).
—Thompson Chain - Bible Book Outlines

Rev 1:1. *Revelation of Yahushua Messiah, which Elohim gave him to show his servants what has to take place with speed. And he signified it by sending his messenger (angel) to his servant John.*

This opening verse shows us that the author is the apostle John, the same John who wrote the Gospel and the three short letters that bear his name. This was his last writing. This verse also shows us that the revelation (singular) is something Elohim gave Yahushua Messiah to show to his servants; that is, believers in him. The whole book is considered as one revelation. It corresponds to the term "the Day of Yahuah." Often people refer to the book as "Revelations," plural. Such people would say, for example, "In Revelations 1:1 it says....." That is incorrect. They should rather say, for example, "In Revelation 1:1 it says......"

The other name for Revelation is Apocalypse, a Greek word that means "revelation, manifestation, appearance." The book in Greek begins with this word. In the book, John records what he saw in a series of events and situations represented in symbolic fashion. Some of the events are repeated under different symbolisms, so not everything is chronological. This book reveals judgment in the end times. Yahushua is coming to bring judgment on the earth because of the wickedness of mankind, and to set up his 1,000 year rule (the Millennium), and his eternal kingdom after the final judgment.

In the book we see a vision of Yahushua with a sword coming out of his mouth to bring judgment (Rev 1).

We see letters to seven assemblies, representing stages of the assembly throughout history, starting from Pentecost with a "first love," and calling them to repent and overcome their sins or be discarded. The sixth assembly is Philadelphia, which represents the overcoming believers at the end of the age who are raptured. The seventh assembly is Laodicea, which represents lukewarm believers who miss the rapture (Rev 2-3).

We see Yahushua seated on a throne opening a scroll with seven seals, each seal representing a judgment (Rev 5-6).

We see 144,000 of twelve tribes of Israel being sealed on their foreheads so as to protect them from harm during the plagues (Rev 7).

We see a male son coming out of a woman and a *drakon* (Gk a large snake) wanting to devour the male son as soon as it is born, the male son representing the last-day perfected bride assembly, the woman representing Babylon, and the *drakon* representing Satan (Rev 12).

We see a beast coming out of the sea and requiring everyone to take its mark, 666, or be killed, representing the anti-messiah (antichrist) world government bringing the great tribulation on all believers who miss the rapture (Rev 13).

We see Babylon the Great, which is the world system, fallen, and seven plagues to bring judgment on the nations for rejecting Yahushua as Messiah and killing all his followers. The last plague is the Battle of Armageddon and the return of Yahushua to destroy all the armies. He throws Satan and his demons into the Abyss for 1,000 years, and begins his 1,000 year rule with only a small remnant of each nation still alive. And we see Satan released after the 1,000 years, another battle against Jerusalem, and then the end of the earth and the universe, and the final judgment of the wicked and the righteous.

We also see the bride of Messiah descending on the new earth, symbolically represented as the New Jerusalem with the throne of Yahuah and Yahushua in her midst.

> Rev 21:22. *And I saw no dwelling place* (temple) *in it, for Yahuah El Shaddai is its Dwelling Place and the Lamb.* [23] *And the city had no need of the sun nor of the moon to shine in it, for the esteem of Elohim lightened it, and the Lamb is its lamp.*

CONCLUSION

THIS HAS BEEN a brief look at the 66 books of scripture, plus the Inter-testament period. The purpose has been to acquaint the readers with a basic understanding of the message so that they will desire to read each book of scripture and dig deeper. These are the words, in writing, of our creator Father, so that we will grow in our love for him and for what he is in his nature of righteousness and purity.

A person in love wants to spend time with the one he loves. It is his highest priority, and so he will schedule his life so as to do it.

The following is from Psalm 19:7-14.

The Torah of Yahuah is perfect, restoring the soul.
> *The testimony of Yahuah is sure, making wise the simple.*
The precepts of Yahuah are right, rejoicing the heart.
> *The commandment of Yahuah is pure, enlightening the eyes.*
The fear of Yahuah is clean, enduring forever.
> *The judgments of Yahuah are true; they are righteous altogether.*
They are more desirable than gold, yes, than much fine gold;
> *Sweeter also than honey and the drippings of the honeycomb.*
Moreover, by them your servant is warned;
> *In keeping them there is great reward.*
Who can discern his errors? Acquit me of hidden faults.
Also keep back your servant from presumptuous sins;
> *Let them not rule over me;*
> *Then I will be blameless,*
> *And I shall be acquitted of great transgression.*
Let the words of my mouth and the meditation of my heart

Be acceptable in your sight,
Yahuah, my rock and my Redeemer (Ps 19:7-14).

ADAM TO ABRAHAM CHART

(Dates are B.C.E. - Before the Common Era)

(Calculation by Dr. Gilbert Olson)

Adam 4004 to 3074 = 930 years

Seth 3874 to 2962 = 912 years

Enosh 3769 to 2864 = 905 years

Kenan 3679 to 2769 = 910 years

Mahalalel 3609 to 2714 = 895 years

Jared 3544 to 2582 = 962 years

Enoch 3382 to 3017 = 365 years

Methuselah 3317 to 2348 = 969 years, year of the flood

Lamech 3130 to 2353 = 777 years

Noah 2948 to 1998 = 950 years

Shem 2445 to 1845 = 600 years

Flood 2348 lasted one year

Arphaxed 2345 to 1872 = 438 years

Shelah 2310 to 1877 = 433 years

Ebar 2280 to 1816 = 464 years

Peleg 2246 to 2007 = 239 years

Reu 2216 to 1977 = 239 years

Serug 2184 to 1954 = 230 years

Nahor 2154 to 2006 = 148 years

Terah 2125 to 1920 = 205 years

Abraham 2055 to 1880 = 175 years

According to this calculation:

Noah was born 126 years after Adam died.

Noah lived to see his descendants fall back into idolatry and the judgment of the languages being confused.

Abraham was 57 years old when Noah died.

Shem lived through the flood and outlived Abraham by 35 years.

Note the decline in how long they lived after the flood.

Books in the Bride of Messiah Series
by Dr Gilbert W Olson

GOD IN MAN
God's Plan of Incarnation

YAHUSHUA MESSIAH, THE LAST ADAM
His Humanity According to Scripture

THE BRIDE AND THE RAPTURE
From Born Again to a Mature Bride

GENESIS
In the Beginning
A Typological Commentary

APOCALYPSE UNVEILED
The Book of Revelation

SURVEY OF THE SCRIPTURES
From Genesis to Revelation
And the Inter-testament Period

Made in the USA
Columbia, SC
21 August 2017